Many Paths to One Fellowship

ItWorks Publishing

gbstebbings@gmail.com

Many Paths to One Fellowship

A narrative timeline of AA history

itWorks Publishing

For information address:

Gary Stebbings

PO Box 1942

Blue Jay, CA 92317

gbstebbings@gmail.com

ISBN-13: 978-1460983652
Printed in the United States of America

Table of Contents

Preface

To put a miracle into words is impossible because miracles are by definition an unexpected event attributed to divine intervention and unable to be adequately given earthly description. With that in mind from the outset, I approached the impossible task of putting into words the miracle of AA's foundation by simply telling a story.

The story that describes the "history" of AA is one that is filled with a long series of synchronistic events. The progression of these "coincidences" slowly builds as time passes and concludes at a "peak moment" when we arrive at a point in time that is now described as the "founding moment".

I begin the story by illustrating America's relationship with alcohol starting with the earliest settlements in the New World. History shows that through the colonial period that relationship grew to become a major problem for our very young nation.

By the early 1800's it became clear that something had to be done and the Temperance movement emerged as a response to the alcoholic epidemic that was sweeping the nation.

By the mid nineteenth century the most successful society in the treatment of alcoholics, The Washingtonians, came forth along with The New Thought Movement. Both of these would have a good deal of influence on Bill W. and the early AA pioneers. The Washingtonians, as Bill discovered in AA's very early days, had made mistakes that AA took measures to avoid.

New Thought affected not only AA but two of the most influential predecessors to AA, the Emmanuel Movement and the Oxford Group.

I also wanted to illustrate how many of the main players in the story affected one another and how much they had in common through a variety of associations and relationships. Throughout the book you will find many examples of the interwoven connections that in complex ways would influence AA and its founders.

The point is this, AA has deep roots that tap into a variety of ancient religions and spiritual movements and it is clear that the history of AA starts long before the meeting between Bill Wilson and Dr. Bob Smith. I hope that as you read the story it will reveal these fascinating synchronicities that lead up to the final founding moment of Alcoholics Anonymous. My hope is that you will become engaged and interested by a story of such important magnitude.

Yours Truly,

Gary Stebbings

Introduction

Living on a one day at time basis allows the recovering alcoholic to focus on the immediate present and what is required to maintain sobriety but this does not allow for the looking back at historical events that affect his present "now". If such an investigation were to made it would offer a look at earlier attempts by those who preceded us in the journey of sobriety and the treatment of alcoholics and drug addicts. We would gain some worthwhile and valuable perspective in the challenges that faced others in their work. The need to learn what worked and what didn't is of great value to our collective future.

In order to reach a particular point in history, people "travel" through a series of life changing events then come to realize where they have been and what happened to them to get to where they are now. Much is the same with groups of people.

This is why I believe that every student of the Big Book of Alcoholics Anonymous (AA) should have a basic knowledge about the history of AA in order to better understand the Book itself. The study of the history of what others had done in prior attempts in the treatment of alcoholics showed Bill W. and early AA members what worked and what did not. Learning where AA came from and studying the experience of other societies and organizations gave them an idea of the obstacles that AA would have to overcome to get a foothold established.

Consider this; it took four years to have an AA membership of "100" and this number included family members and newcomers whose sobriety was shaky at best. When Bill began writing the Big Book he had just over four years. The average length of sobriety for those who contributed to the writing was about 18 months. All were relative newcomers by today's standards[1]. What they lacked in experience was overcome by looking back at what others had done before them. The Emmanuel Movement and Richard Peabody had just come to an end only several years before AA. This group served as a virtual seedbed for early AA. Together with an offshoot of the Emmanuel Movement, the Jacoby club, Bill W. had an excellent source of proven methods. Both the Emmanuel Movement and the Jacoby club have been recognized as important predecessors to AA. They demonstrated the importance of fellowship and established that a spiritual conversion was the only way to lasting sobriety.

The student of AA history will soon realize what a miracle it truly is to have AA emerge at time in history when the states of affairs were just right for AA to make its entrance. A chain of synchronistic events had to occur for AA's initial success.

It is the authors hope that the reader of this book will find a golden thread of synchronistic events that illustrate where AA came from and how it got to where it is now. The reader will see that as the first pilgrims walked onto the shores of Plymouth, Mass., they were planting seeds from which our predecessors would harvest the ingredients necessary to pave the Path to the Fellowship of AA. Throughout America's history people and groups came forward to contribute to the path, sometimes in very obvious ways and sometimes in very subtle ways.

Many paths had to be traveled before the world was ready to receive a new and revolutionary way of treating the alcoholic. AA had to wait for a time when a convergence of philosophical thought, religious and spiritual beliefs had matured and the world was ready for the entrance of a group (AA) that utilized these new ideas and a new spiritual approach to the treatment of alcoholics. Without the necessary growth of the human race in general, AA would have never been accepted.

Without knowing where we came from we are apt to forget to remember and be doomed to the same fate as other movements. Over confidence and diluting their purpose were fatal flaws to many that preceded AA. The AA traditions that have kept the fellowship on course were not developed by other groups and without these simple guidelines they lost their way, which led in time to their demise.

Many individuals that had tremendous influence on the development and formation of AA had to be educated and prepared for the roles that they played. The main players had to progress sufficiently in their disease to qualify for their roles. Institutions and organizations had to be established and ready for the entrance of the main cast. It is only after the stage is set and every player had been prepared will the curtain open and the audience is ready for AA to have its success guaranteed.

Many Paths had to be followed to one fellowship.

Gary Stebbings 2011

Part 1- Colonial America 1618-1784

1618

The first law to control the use of alcohol was made in Virginia

Founded in 1607, some 13 years before the Pilgrims landed in Plymouth, Jamestown served as the capital of Virginia throughout the 17th century and saw the establishment of the language, customs, laws and government practiced in our nation today.

Serious problems soon emerged in the small English outpost, which was located in the midst of a chiefdom of about 14,000 Algonquian-speaking Indians ruled by the powerful leader Powhatan. Relations with the Powhatan Indians were tenuous, although trading opportunities were established. An unfamiliar climate, as well as brackish water supply and lack of food (conditions possibly aggravated by a prolonged drought) led to disease and death. Many of the original colonists were upper-class Englishmen, and the colony lacked sufficient laborers and skilled farmers.

The lack of clean drinkable water was a public health problem as it was in Europe and fostered the consumption of alcoholic beverages because alcohol killed bacteria. The colony of Jamestown simply could not consume the available water safely and thus the seeds of America's relationship with alcohol found fertile soil[1].

The use of alcohol was prevalent as it was in Europe during this period. Its consumption was not looked down upon although drunkenness was. An individual was permitted to drink all that they wanted as long as it did not interfere with their work or other duties. The first Laws to control the use of alcohol were written at this time and stated that it was illegal to be publically intoxicated and alcohol should not keep the user from performing their customary duties.

Public floggings and wearing of the drunkards cloak were the punishment for drunkards.

The Drunkards Cloak.

SUPPLICE DU GRAND KNOUT.

1621

Plymouth, Mass. – the Stage is Set

Plymouth Colony was an English colonial venture in North America from 1620 to 1691. The first settlement of the Plymouth Colony was at New Plymouth, a location previously surveyed and named by Captain John Smith. The settlement, which served as the capital of the colony, is today the modern town of Plymouth, Massachusetts. At its height, Plymouth Colony occupied most of the southeastern portion of the modern state of Massachusetts.

In the winter of 1621, the Mayflower was anchored at Plymouth harbor. The colonists lived aboard the vessel while shelter was being built on land. A devastating "general sickness" brought about by exposure, malnutrition, scurvy, pneumonia and other life threatening illnesses was widespread among these brave souls. Death was common and ever present[2].

The Mayflower

A safe water supply

At this point in history alcohol was still safer than water to drink on a daily basis. In 17th century Europe, the water was frequently spoiled and contained disease causing bacteria. The Pilgrim colonists anticipated the same when they arrived in America. Spirits and beer kept well while making the long voyage across the sea. Water would become foul in wooden barrels and would be disease laden.

The Consumption of alcoholic beverages was a vital and necessary part of life for the Pilgrim colonists who did not understand that water could also be a beverage. It was at this point in American history that our dependence on alcohol was established and over the next several generations this dependence would progress into a widespread social problem that would ultimately be addressed by the Temperance movement of the 1830's[2].

Shortage of Beer supply creates crisis

During the first winter in the New World, the Mayflower colonists suffered greatly from diseases like scurvy, lack of shelter and general conditions onboard ship. Forty-five of the One hundred and two emigrants died the first winter and were buried on Cole's Hill. Additional deaths during the first year meant that only fifty three people were alive in November 1621.

To top things off they were running out of beer which was literally their life's blood. The pilgrim's supply of beer was at a perilously low point and a crisis was looming. The sailors that had to return to Europe were in fear that if they allowed the settlers to consume all their beer supply they would have insufficient supply for the trip back. They were not willing to take that risk for it meant life or death to them.

William Bradford

Bradford, William, 1590–1657,

The Governor of Plymouth Colony, born, Austerfield, Yorkshire, England. As a young man he joined the separatist congregation at Scrooby and in 1609 immigrated with others to Holland, where, at Leiden, he acquired a wide acquaintance with theological literature. Bradford came to New England on the *Mayflower* in 1620 and in 1621,

The situation reaches a climax

As the situation came to a climax William Bradford the Governor of Massachusetts told the pilgrims to move ashore and drink the plentiful and available water on land. Governor Bradford pleaded with the sailors for a small supply of beer which brought forth refusal on the part of the sailors. It was a sad beginning for the new colonists. The suffering caused by lack of beer and a safe water source mercifully became too much and the Captain of the Mayflower relented by sending a modest supply of beer for those that needed it most, the sick and the dying. This humanitarian act assured the settlers who were facing the "starving time" during the first winter they would at least have an occasional life saving taste of the old world. In short time the Pilgrims would be able to brew their own supply of beer, fortifying them and providing a healthy drinking source[2].

1633

Drunkenness as a punishable crime

In Plymouth Colony, 1633, John Holmes was censured for drunkenness: his penalty was to "sit in the stocks, and was amerced forty shillings."

First time offenders were put in the stocks. Repeat offenders were sentenced to hard labor or Corporal punishment.

Cider, beer, and wine were the drinks of choice. The Puritans believed alcohol was God's gift to man, and a test of his soul. "The wine is from God, but the drunkard is from the Devil". (Puritan aphorism)

Tithingmen (tax-collectors) oversaw ten-families each, monitored excessive drunkenness and reported it to the minister, who reported it to the Governor's representative. Ministers could punish first time offenders, but repeat offenders were sent to the governor's representative for punishment[1].

When people broke the law in colonial Virginia, the courts ordered swift and often public punishments. Many of these punishments would be strange or harsh to Americans today. Unlike today, jails were used as places to hold people accused of crimes until they were brought to trial. They were not used as places for punishment. However, if the court imposed a fine, but the defendant could not pay, he sometimes spent time in jail until he did pay the fine in full.

1662

The First American Beverages

The pilgrims soon set about the task of making their own alcoholic beverages. They used indigenous plants and also planted European fruits in order to make apple jack, mead, and peach brandy.

When the Mayflower set sail for the return trip to Europe, the most popular brew was a dark hearty beverage that contained about 6% alcohol that was brewed from barley malt flavored with hops and this evolved into the modern porter and stout beers.

John Winthrop Jr., then Governor of Connecticut and the son of Governor John Winthrop of Massachusetts, brewed a very tasty brew from Indian corn. This unique contribution led to the younger Winthrop being elected to the Royal Society of London. This was a high honor for they considered it a contribution to the advancement of science[3].

During this time period gin brought over from England, by soldiers returning from duty in Holland was consumed in large quantities. It was distilled with little expense from grain spirits and flavored by the juniper berry. Gin drinking grew to an alarming extent and was completely out of control by 1740.

Gin has a dubious reputation in America and remained a spirit with negative connotations until the 20th century when it was mixed with vermouth and olives to form the martini.

The backyard still, otherwise known as "Limbecs", became part of the landscape. Pears were used to distill a beverage called "perry" and settlers in Vermont distilled honey to produce mead.

Gin Lane - London 1740

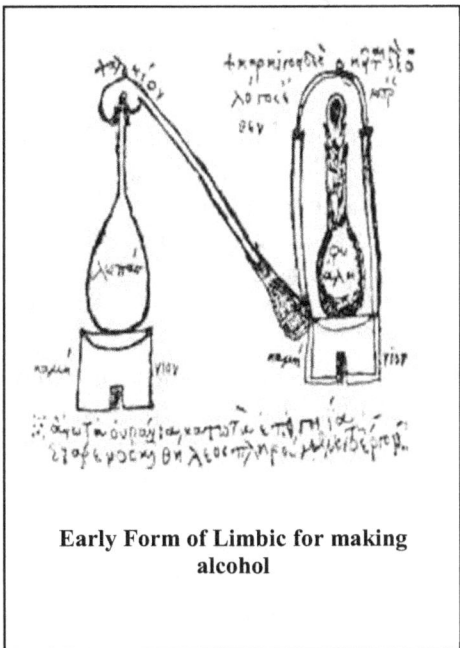

Early Form of Limbic for making alcohol

1720

Early use and abuse

By this time the local tavern has emerged as a gathering place for politicians, militia, and artisans. The Anglican and Puritan Churches used wine in their communion services. The use of alcohol in many forms was pervasive and was consumed by both genders and all ages.

Politicians seeking office provided generous quantities of alcohol to win over the electorate. The use and consumption of "spirits" was ever present at polling places. The voters of this time had to make long trips to the county poll and came to expect a drink at the end of their journey. The founding fathers provided copious amounts of libation to their supporters[2].

Militia drills that were crucial to the settlers' welfare were often reduced in effectiveness by the heavy consumption of liquor. The drills were known as little more that social gatherings where drinking alcoholic beverages in large amounts was a primary aspect. A completely sober militia drill was highly unusual and when one occurred on the Boston Commons the Massachusetts governor, John Winthrop, was greatly pleased.

Prior to the American Revolution taverns and inns were favorite places to hold political debates. They also served as a formation point for the militia and as a recruiting station for General Washington's Continental Army[3].

It is impossible to calculate accurate figures of the amount of alcohol consumed, but estimates suggest that during the 1790's the average American over age 15, drank 5.8 gallons of distilled spirits , 34 gallons of beer and cider, as well as a gallon of wine each year. (This represents a huge volume of absolute alcohol when you consider the average American citizen today consumes less than 2.9 gallons annually.)[3]

Generally the American colonist was apathetic towards this rampant alcohol use. Little if any outcry was generated by the citizens at large. This general lack of concern was a prominent attitude among the colonists.

1750

The social norms surrounding alcohol consumption were left unchecked by society and citizen's behavior had become so loose that politicians like John Adams of Massachusetts, expressed concern over the abusive consumption of alcohol. He focused the thrust of his outrage at the taverns that had now become drunken whore houses. The local tavern attracted the urban poor who consumed excessive amounts of alcohol and participated in gambling and prostitution. It was becoming more and more evident that something had to be done to put a restraint on this behavior.

1774

Anthony Benezet- authored the first written assault on the abuse of alcohol

A response to the ever worsening sacred decay came from Anthony Benezet. He was a Philadelphia Quaker, who published the first written assault on the unhealthy and disturbing drinking habits that existed in colonial America. His timely essay – "The Mighty Destroyer Displayed" illustrated in graphic form the degrading and immoral behavior that alcohol brought about. It was read by a large percentage of literate colonists but its impact was hard to determine. By 1784, Quaker and Methodist Churches were urging their congregations to abstain from hard liquor, its sale and distribution[5].

This American philanthropist and Quaker educator, Anthony Benezet (1713-1784) was among the earliest civil rights activists; in addition, he promoted education for women and supported women's rights. He also was for improving relations with Native Americans. Mr. Benezet wrote antislavery essays and distributed them in Colonial America.

Concerned about slavery in America, he corresponded with English emancipationists and began to regularly write articles for newspapers and almanacs on this subject.

Anthony Benezet

Anthony Benezet was born in Saint-Quentin, France, on 31 January 1713.
His family were Huguenots. Because of the persecution of Protestants after the revocation of the Edict of Nantes in 1685, his family decided to leave France. They moved first to Rotterdam, then briefly to Greenwich, then to London. In 1727 Benezet joined the Religious Society of Friends. In 1731 the Benezet family immigrated to Philadelphia, Pennsylvania, in North America.

Distressed by the poor education opportunities available for women, he established a girl's school in 1755. Benezet health being poor, he decided to retire to his wife's hometown in Burlington, NJ. After which he wrote: "A Caution; to Great Britain and Her Colonies on the calamitous state of the Enslaved Negroes" in 1766. This came to be his most important work and was widely distributed in England. He helped stir up English protests against the slave trade by writing "His Some Historical Account of Guinea in 1771". He also had founded a school for African American children in 1770 and after the American Revolution, the school met in his home.

Convinced that Native Americans had been abused and mistreated, he worked to improve their treatment. To bring this situation to the public's attention, he published, "Some Observations of Indian Natives of this Continent". Yet the issues involving African Americans, Women's rights, and Native Americans were not his only concerns, alcohol and its affects still haunted him and many Americans. His previous essay was having an impact[5].

Part 2 – The Growing problem and Americas response 1784-1872

1784

Dr. Benjamin Rush-A Voice of Reason

Dr. Benjamin Rush, born in Philadelphia, PA, was a member of the Continental Congress and a signer of the Declaration of Independence. He served as the Surgeon General of the Continental Army during the American Revolution. Dr. Rush is considered by many as the "Father of American Psychiatry" and as he is more widely known, "The Father of the American Temperance Movement". He is among the earliest of prominent Americans to bring attention to the seriousness of the "disease" of Alcoholism. Dr. Rush read and was alerted by Anthony Benezet's essay on "American Drinking Habits and their Deleterious Effects on Society", Rush responded by writing, "An Inquiry into the Effects of Ardent Spirits on the Human Body and Mind". Written from his position as a medical doctor, he described habitual drunkenness as a "progressive and odious disease"[1].

In 1810, Dr. Rush proposed the creation of "sober houses" where alcoholics could be confined and rehabilitated. He observed that "ardent spirits" consumed chronically in large amounts destroyed a person's health and could cause irreversible liver damage and death. He also described an addiction process as a "craving" and identified alcohol as the addictive agent. Dr. Rush stated that, "Once addicted, even a saint would have a hard time controlling himself."[1] In a matter of words, he is describing the "allergy" that Dr. William D. Silkworth brought forth and described in the book, "Alcoholics Anonymous", "The Doctor's Opinion".

Dr. Rush was among the first to assert that complete abstinence was the only effective treatment for alcoholism.

Benjamin Rush (January 4, 1746 – April 19, 1813) was a Founding Father of the United States. Rush lived in the state of Pennsylvania and was a physician, writer, educator, humanitarian and a Universalist, as well as the founder of Dickinson College in Carlisle, Pennsylvania.

He was a staunch opponent of Gen. George Washington and worked tirelessly to have him removed as the Commander-In-Chief of the Continental Army. Later in life, he became a professor of medical theory and clinical practice at the University of Pennsylvania. Despite having a wide influence on the development of American government, he is not as widely known as many of his American contemporaries. Rush was also an early opponent of slavery and capital punishment.

The USS CONSTITUTION

The USS Constitution is the oldest warship remaining in the United Sates naval fleet. It was ordered to be built by George Washington in 1797.

To provide an adequate drinking supply of water became a challenge on long voyages. Fresh water taken on board in casks quickly spoiled and developed a slimy consistency from the algae it contained. The practice of sweetening the stagnant water using beer or wine was used to make the water more palatable.

As sea voyages became longer the stowage of large numbers of casks of beer or wine became difficult adding weight to the vessel. Following the British conquest of Jamaica in 1655, rum replaced the beer and became the drink of choice. The daily ration of grog dates back over two hundred years and developed as a way of ensuring a safe supply of drinking water to the sailors[4].

During The Revolutionary War:

She set sail from Boston, on 23 August, 1779, with 475 officers and men, 48,600 gallons of fresh water, 7,400 cannon shot, 11,600 pounds of black powder, and 79,400 gallons of rum on board. Her mission was to destroy and harass English shipping.

Making Jamaica on 6 October, she took on 826 pounds of flour and 68,300 gallons of rum. Then headed for the Azores, arriving there on 12 November, She provisioned with 550 pounds of beef and 64,300 gallons of Portuguese wine.

On the 18th of November she set sail for England. In the ensuing day, she defeated five British Men-of-War and captured and scuttled twelve English Merchant-Men, salvaging only their rum.

By 27 January 1780, her powder and shot were exhausted. Unarmed, she made a raid up the Firth of Clyde. Her landing party captured a whiskey distillery and transferred 40,000 gallons to board by dawn. Then she headed home. The Constitution arrived in Boston harbor on 20 February, l780, with no cannon shot, no powder, no food, no rum, no whiskey, but with 48,600 gallons of stagnant water.

[Excerpted from U.S. Naval Institute Proceedings]
Note: Ships are commonly referred to in the female gender

Note: By 1790, the estimated alcohol consumption of each adult was six gallons of absolute alcohol per year (2.5 oz. alcohol/adult/day) - twice the estimated level of alcohol consumption in America I 1985.

1790's

The American Temperance Movement is born

From the late 1700's to the early 1800's, alcohol consumption and the number of distilleries and breweries increased tremendously. A growing movement spearheaded by prominent citizens such as, George Washington, Thomas Jefferson, Ben Franklin and John Adams and fueled by Dr. Rush's essay on alcoholism began calling for the citizens to change their drinking habits. Religious leaders pushed for total abstinence thus the beginning of the "American Temperance Movement"[3].

1820's

Alcohol consumption is reaching alarming amounts

At this time People in the United States were consuming 27 liters (7 gallons) of pure alcohol per capita annually. Political and religious leaders were viewing drunkenness as a national epidemic.

The American Temperance Movement

Protestant clergymen believe that temperance was the only way to obtain salvation and save the soul. God as the solution to the alcoholic problem was established. The widespread view that God or a religious conversion experience could relieve alcoholism was new and would have a permanent influence on a long series of individuals. In 1826, in Boston, Lyman Beecher and Justin Edwards spearheaded the founding of "The American Society for the Promotion of Temperance". By 1836, the society had grown and was renamed, "The American Temperance Society" (ATS). Their constitution stated that in order to produce a lasting change of public opinion and to alter the habits and traditions of the people the outcome of temperance with all of its many attributes must prevail[3].

Lyman Beecher

American Temperance Society

The American Society for the Promotion of Temperance or better known as the **American Temperance Society (ATS)** was a society established on February 13, 1826 in Boston, MA. Within five years there were 2,220 local chapters in the U.S. with 170,000 members who had taken a pledge to abstain from drinking distilled beverages. Within ten years, there were over 8,000 local groups and more than 1,500,000 members who had taken the pledge.

1830 – The movement takes hold

Prior to this period of time "temperance" was not a popular cause however the need was so great and even laws that were enacted did not help a great deal to stop the public menace that was ubiquitous.

The Temperance movements began to take hold. Starting in 1829 there were by one count 1000 individual societies throughout the United States. In five short years there were 5,000 societies established claiming 11,000,000 members. When the "American Temperance Union" in 1836 decided to take the unpopular stand of "Total Abstinence" from all forms of intoxicants, it was not surprising that approximately 2,000 societies and countless individuals retreated from the movement. Wealthy supporters and leaders withdrew their support as they were unwilling to abstain from wine and beer. Many became discouraged by the resistance and hostility to the new pledge of total abstinence and became inactive and the movement's progress faltered. By 1840 the movement that had once flourished was falling on lean times. Efforts to revitalize the movement were limited and fruitless[4].

As for the active alcoholic or drunkard, the prevailing opinion was that little could be done to help them. There existed a general pessimism as to the possibility of rehabilitating drunkards. All efforts were aimed at keeping nonalcoholics from becoming alcoholics and this meant stopping the cause of alcoholism which was thought to be alcohol.

It was at this point the stage was set for the emergence of groups and individuals with new ways of thinking and new ways of treating the alcoholic.

The Drunkards Progress

THE DRUNKARDS PROGRESS

The Steps of the Drunkards Progress

Step 1: A glass with a friend.
Step 2: A glass to keep the cold out.
Step 3: A glass too much.
Step 4: Drunk and riotous.
Step 5: The summit attained.
Step 6: Poverty and disease.
Step 7: Forsaken by friends.
Step 8: Desperation and crime.
Step 9: Death by suicide.

1840

The Washingtonian Movement

The Washingtonian Temperance Society otherwise known as the Washingtonian Movement (WM) was formed on Thursday evening, April 2, 1840 when six drinking buddies (William Mitchell, John Hoss, David Anderson, George Steers, James McCurley and Archibald Campbell) met at Chasel's Tavern in Baltimore, MD., and formed a total abstinence society. They named themselves the *Washington Temperance Society* (in honor of George Washington). They later became known as *Washingtonians*[1].

The group, on a whim, went to listen to a well known Temperance Leader speak. Afterward they discussed the lecture, one of the group suggested half jokingly that they form a total abstinence society and on April 5 the six men decided that they "drink no more of the poisonous draft, forever".

They each agreed to bring another (newcomer) to their next meeting. After this they penned a pledge not to "drink any spirituous or malt liquors, wine or cider". They named their newly formed movement the Washington Temperance Society in honor of George Washington who had the reputation of being a modest drinker.

The meetings continued to be held at Chasel's Tavern until the owner's wife pointed out to her husband that they were losing their best customers. After being asked to meet elsewhere by the tavern owner, they met at a members home until they were able to rent a meeting hall. They continued meeting and bringing in new members. The society proved to be such a success that on the first anniversary, their membership had risen to a count of about 1000 members[2].

This incredible growth was in part due to excellent timing and filling a tremendous need in the drunkard's possibilities for recovery. In addition, several leaders turned out to be powerful speakers. They traveled widely spreading the message, speaking to ever larger crowds and signing many new members who took the oath and then brought new members themselves. It was all the rage to sign the pledge and be a Washingtonian member.

By May of 1842, the WM had spread to every major city in the country and had particularly strong followings in New York and New England. At its hay day, the movement estimated its membership to be in the area of one to six million total members and among them 100,000 to 600,000 actual sober alcoholics. The society claimed to have sobered up every conceivable type of alcoholic and its ranks were swollen by family members as well. Similar to AA at its formation, the entire family attended meetings for recovery and support[2].

 An important branch was the formed and became known as the "Martha Washington" society which fed the poor, clothed the naked and reclaimed the sobriety of women.

Timothy Shay Arthur In 1840 wrote a series of newspaper articles on the Washingtonian Temperance Society, a local organization formed by working-class artisans and mechanics to counter the life-ruining effects of alcohol. The articles were widely reprinted and helped fuel the establishment of Washingtonian groups across the country. Arthur's newspaper sketches were collected in book form as *Six Nights with the Washingtonians* (1842). *Six Nights* went through many editions and helped establish Arthur in the public eye as an author associated with the temperance movement.

1842 Abraham Lincoln Speaks to the Springfield, IL

On Feb 22, 1842, Mr. Lincoln spoke and praised the WM and basically scolded earlier temperance movements and individuals that degraded the alcoholic and declared them incorrigible[2].

Abraham Lincoln

"I believe if we take habitual drunkards as a class, their heads and their hearts will bear an advantageous comparison with those of any other class. There seems ever to have been proneness in the brilliant ant warm blooded to fall into this vice." Lincoln is also quoted as saying that intoxicating liquor was "used by everybody, repudiated by nobody" and that it came forth in society "like the Egyptian angel of death commissioned to slay if not the first, the fairest born in every family."

Abraham Lincoln Feb. 22, 1842

1843

The WM Peaks

By this time, the WM peaked after spreading to all major areas of the United States. An accurate account of membership is impossible. One of its major flaws resided in the fact that the only requirement for membership was to sign the pledge. Its combined membership included non-drinkers, religious leaders, politicians and drinkers of all types that weren't alcoholics by admission or behavior. Their ranks consisted of far more "normal drinkers" than alcoholics with the allergy. It was impossible to arrive at the number of rehabilitated alcoholics but an estimate was less than 150,000 over the life of the movement[3].

1847

All but gone in a few short years

It is a sad testimony that the WM peaked and was all but gone in a few short years. When they formed, the Washingtonians were tied in many ways to the faltering temperance movement that began in the 1820's. At their beginning the movement was noted for their different treatment of the alcoholic. They treated the alcoholic as you would a sick person with love and kindness; they won over the drunk with what they called "moral suasion".

The Washingtonians drifted away from their initial purpose of helping the individual alcoholic. Disagreements, controversies and infighting destroyed what was at one time a beneficial resource to the problem drinker. The WM's good work perished in the swirl of controversy over temperance and prohibition. Their successes, which might have benefitted untold thousands of alcoholics, perished along with them.

The main difference between the Washingtonians and the Temperance Movement was that the Washingtonians goal was to treat the individual where as the Temperance's goal was to change societies drinking habits and ultimately create the prohibition of alcohol[2].

Early Washingtonian meeting descriptions draw remarkable resemblance to today's AA meetings as their practices were similar. Like AA, they told their stories or witnessed, giving a personal account of their experience with alcohol. This practice was particularly successful when public meetings drew large crowds and this was a way to keep them interesting. Just like AA meetings, only the alcoholic or ex-drunk could share. This measure was written into the Washingtonian Charter as they tried to establish a tradition where the message could be carried from one drunk to another. At the start, debates, lectures and speeches were not permitted. Politics and religion were both subjects that were avoided so as all would feel free to become members. They began with one purpose and that was to help the alcoholic who suffered from the terrible disease of alcoholism.

1848

The movement strayed from its initial primary purpose

Despite getting off to a phenomenal start, the WM had simply "destroyed itself completely and dropped out of sight... and with it went the hopes it had held out for thousands of drunks of that day", and by 1852, all that remained of their spectacular but short lived movement was its home for the fallen in Boston, Massachusetts.

Certain similarities between the WM of the nineteenth century and the present day fellowship of Alcoholics Anonymous have been commented upon by a number of observers. In view of this resemblance there was more than a historical interest regarding this first movement in the United States which brought about a large-scale rehabilitation of alcoholics. The phenomenal rise and spread of the

WM throughout the land in the early 1840's provided the occasion for much discussion, exciting a deep interest. The cause of its equally rapid decline has been a subject for much speculation and is still of concern to some members of Alcoholics Anonymous who may wonder whether or not AA is destined to a similar fate[2].

When you weigh the evidence it becomes clear, in short order, just how and why the WM came to an abrupt end. Their demise was due to the WM's lack of guiding principles such as those used in the Twelve Traditions of AA. The WM strayed from its intended singleness of purpose and violated almost every principle incorporated into the Twelve Traditions.

The Washingtonians strayed from their primary purpose of helping the alcoholic. Along with this came arguing, fighting, and their entrance into outside issues. Learning from this, AA adopted the 5th tradition that states; "Each group has but one primary purpose to carry its message to the alcoholic that still suffers". In addition to this major blunder, the WM never developed a program for personality and spiritual change like the 12 Steps of AA. Their approach to the disease was moralistic rather than spiritual change or conversion. Working with other alcoholics was not a requirement of WM members, unlike AA's 12th Step that states;"...we tried to carry this message to alcoholics..." There was no anonymity in practice that would keep public awareness away from of those members that relapsed or from members that would use the movement for personal gains.

The Sixth tradition was put into practice in AA to avoid situations whereby members would gain prestige and fame as well as receive monetary compensation for any purpose. It states; "An AA group ought never endorse, finance or lend the AA name..."

Finally the WM made strenuous efforts to avoid or minimize sectarian, theological, political disputes and differences in beliefs. In the end, they could not avoid attracting hostile forces and violent emotional outbreaks brought out by these conflicts.

In "The Grapevine" (an AA newsletter) an article written in August, 1945, Bill reflected on the lessons to be learned from the WM and emphasized to AA's the importance of being "...strong enough and single purposed enough...". Although many wish to make comparisons between the WM and AA, in many ways the WM's have more in common with modern rehabs and recovery groups that are non-religious and do not emphasize a spiritual recovery. Perhaps their greatest liability was that they did not seek divine help for their cause...

In the late 1940s through 1950, AA formed the Twelve Traditions which are the principles that guide the AA groups from such pitfalls as those that befell the Washingtonians. The lesson learned from the demise of the Washingtonians was that AA needed to avoid outside, controversial, non-AA issues, thus establishing a tradition of "singleness of purpose."

Origins of Alcoholics Anonymous twelve traditions

The publication of *Alcoholics Anonymous* was in 1939 and by 1944, the number of AA groups had grown along with the number of letters being sent to the AA headquarters in New York asking how to handle disputes caused by issues like , membership, publicity, religion, and finances.

By 1946 AA cofounder Bill Wilson had derived basic ideas for the Twelve Traditions directly from such correspondence with groups, setting guidelines on how groups and members should interact with each other, the public, and AA as a whole.

The Traditions were first published in the April 1946 AA Grapevine under the title *Twelve Points to Assure Our Future*[1] and were formally adopted at AA's First International Convention in 1950. Wilson's book on the subject, *Twelve Steps and Twelve Traditions*, was published in 1953

1838

The Emergence of the New Thought Movement

At this time in American History, as pointed out earlier, there existed a tremendous need for help with the alcohol problem. It is interesting to note that just as the WM was being formed, the New Thought Movement was (almost simultaneously) approaching the alcohol problem and health issues of all types.

Americans were consuming alcohol beverages in unbridled amounts. Drunkards congregated in taverns in droves, the society as a whole was suffering. Unlike many European countries who looked to the government to solve a problem, Americans, had developed the practice of seeing a problem and doing something about it. Churches and community groups often led the way. At precisely this time as if on cue there was a convergence of philosophical thought and groups emerged to take on this menacing problem.

New Thought Movement (NT) dates back to the "dawn of mankind", however, a resurgence of New Thought came forth at this time in America. The Movement was/is a spiritual method developed during the mid to late 19th century. It emphasized metaphysical beliefs and promoted the theory that "infinite intelligence" or "God" was everywhere and in everything. Divine thought was considered as a force for good and all illness originated in the mind. "Right thinking" had a healing effect[4].

NT taught all to recognize that humans were triune beings; Spiritual, Mental and Physical. An acceptable teaching or philosophy must, out of necessity, satisfy all aspects of our being.

They believed that as spiritual beings, mankind sought something that would satisfy the cosmic senses (where man belonged in the spiritual scheme of things). Mankind's need to feel part of the universal creator was a primary quest.

As mental beings, ideas and philosophy were rational and scientifically verifiable and not an affront to the intellect; it should make sense.

As physical, emotional beings, mankind needed to experience something emotionally satisfying; something that was felt; something that permeated our entire being[1].

This type of thinking had great appeal to Bill W. who as evidenced in his own story had trouble with a concept of God. New thought must have helped Bill develop the mind body spirit aspect of the disease of alcoholism as he wrote in Chapter 5..."for we have been not only mentally and physically ill, we have been spiritually sick."

Phineas P. Quimby- Founding Father of New Thought in America (February 16, 1802 – January 16, 1866)

Quimby was given the credit as the founding father of New Thought in America. He was a New England clock maker by trade who became interested in Mesmerism that was the fore-runner of hypnotism today (a new phenomenon brought over from France in 1838). The technique as postulated by Franz Mesmer appeared to affect cures to gravely ill patients who were beyond the help of medicine. Quimby researched these phenomena and received a personal "miraculous" healing. He determined that this technique did not require scientific verification to cure. Quimby was one of the first to attempt a method of healing by using what he termed as the "science of Christ" or "Christ Science". His assumption was that he had rediscovered the method employed by Jesus in his healings. He was credited by many for healing several thousand gravely ill patients that were "incurable" by the medical establishment at that time[2].

Phineas P. Quimby

MY THEORY: "the trouble is in the mind, for the body is only the house for the mind to dwell in . . . If your mind has been deceived by some invisible enemy into a belief; you have put it into the form of a disease, with or without your knowledge. By my theory or truth I come in contact with your enemy and restore you to health and happiness". Phineas P.Quimby

In 1838, Quimby began studying Mesmerism after attending a lecture by Doctor Collyer and soon began further experimentation with the help of Lucius Burkmar, who could fall into a trance and diagnose illnesses. Quimby again saw the mental and placebo effect of the mind over the body when medicines prescribed by Burkmar, with no physical value, cured patients of diseases. From the conclusions of these studies; Phineas Quimby developed theories of mentally aided healing and opened an office in Portland, Maine in 1859[2].

Franz Anton Mesmer was the Austrian physician after whom mesmerism was named, a famously flamboyant believer in the healing powers of an unknown physical property he dubbed "animal magnetism." He enjoyed a popular following and claimed to be able to "channel" magnetic powers in order to cure a variety of ailments, which he did for public display.

Quimby developed seven elements for his theory.

1. The omnipresent Wisdom, the warm, loving Father of us all, Creator of all the universe, whose works are good, whose substance is an invisible reality.

2. The real man, whose life is eternal in the invisible kingdom of God, whose senses are spiritual and function independently of matter.

3. The visible world, which Dr. Quimby once characterized as "the shadow of Wisdom's amusements"; that is, nature is only the outward projection or manifestation of an inward activity far more real and enduring.

4. Spiritual matter, or fine interpenetrating substance, directly responsive to thought and subconsciously embodying in the flesh the fears, beliefs, hopes, errors, and joys of the mind.

5. Disease is due to false reasoning in regard to sensations, which man unwittingly develops by
impressing wrong thoughts and mental pictures upon the subconscious spiritual matter.

6. As disease is due to false reasoning, so health is due to knowledge of the truth. To remove disease permanently, it is necessary to know the cause, the error which led to it. "The explanation is the cure."

7. To know the truth about life is therefore the sovereign remedy for all ills. This truth Jesus came to declare. Jesus knew how he cured and Dr. Quimby, without taking any credit to himself as a discoverer, believed that he understood and practiced the same great truth or science[2].

Early New Thought Practitioners

Mary Eddy Baker

One of Quimby's best known patients who was cured through his method was Mary Baker Eddy. His "medicine free" healing techniques had a profound influence on her. While under his care, she became deeply interested in Quimby's methods and his theory of disease and it's treatment[3].

Mary Baker Eddy (July 16, 1821 – December 3, 1910)

She was the founder of Christian Science and was widely recognized outside her church as one of the most remarkable religious leaders of the era. Much of her childhood and her adult life was spent in ill health. She spent many years looking for healing in many methods available in her time. She had a profound interest in the subject of God's healing power. She wrote "Science and Health" with key to the scriptures that according to Lois Wilson was read by Bill only months before his last admission to Townes Hospital where he had his "white light" spiritual experience[12].

Among the other patients and students who were treated by Quimby and joined with him in his research were Warren Felt Evans, Annetta Seaburg Dresser and Julius Dresser, who helped him, put his teachings into writing[2].

Warren Felt Evans

Warren Felt Evans not only healed but wrote a great deal. His great distinction was that he was the first to write about the New Thought theory of healing as taught and practiced by Quimby.

His first book, *The Mental Cure, (Illustrating the Influence of the Mind on the Body, Both in Health and Disease, and the Psychological Method of Treatment,)* was published in 1869, only three years after Quimby's death and six years before the appearance of *Science & Health* by Mrs. Eddy. Thus, Evans became the first in a long line of authors to write about New Thought ideas and methods[7].

He joined the Church of the New Jerusalem (Swedenborgian), after having read the works of the great Swedish seer, Emanuel Swedenborg. He later converted to the religion. (Authors Note: Later Lois and Bill Wilson would also join this church).

Annetta and Julius Dresser

Annetta G. Seabury Dresser
Lent by Dorothea Reyes

Annetta and Julius Dresser

Julius and Annetta Dresser were early practitioners of the healing methods taught and practiced by Phineas Parkhurst Quimby.

In most respects it is clear that the Dressers follow closely the theory and practice of Quimby, however they gave the impression of a kind of religious warmth in them that goes beyond anything in Quimby's teachings. They taught that "God is omnipresent wisdom, immanent in all the universe and man. Every man possesses in some degree God within. Indeed, man has no good quality or power that is wholly his own, rather all that he possesses is God within. All the qualities of love, mercy, justice, and truth that reside in man, though they are but a spark of the infinite love, or mercy, or justice, or wisdom"[4].

Annetta Dresser published a book in 1895 entitled *The Philosophy of P. P. Quimby* giving a historical sketch of the life and works of P. P. Quimby and outling the healing methods that he taught.

William James

In *The Varieties of Religious Experience:* (1902), William James offers a sense of validity to the formerly abstract idea of spiritual experience. With an understanding of physiology, psychology, and philosophy, James studied cases of religious inspiration and concluded that there were specific aspects of human consciousness that contained energies that could come to a person's assistance in time of great need. The result is what he refers to as the religious experience[9].

Trained in chemistry and medicine, James looked at religious experience as a scientist might, by researching many case studies. However, his theories about religious experience were also heavily influenced by his philosophical interests, which drew him to conclude that an unseen reality does exist and is available to everyone for exploration. His sentiments were somewhat aligned with the beliefs of the transcendentalists, with his work honoring the individual rather than the institutions of religion.

The Varieties of Religious Experience is actually a collection of lectures James delivered in Edinburgh, Scotland. The lectures were sponsored by Adam Gifford, who was interested in promoting a series of studies of what he referred to as a natural theology[9]. James's lectures became by far the most popular in the series. James also received international attention and praise as one of the first American philosophers to have his ideas welcomed and respected in Europe. Although not cited as James's best book, *The Varieties of Religious Experience* continues to be referred to as one of the best books on religion.

In his day, intellectuals tended to categorize religious experiences as no more than a nervous condition or a reaction caused by indigestion. *The Varieties of Religious Experience* portrays the need for a sense of the spiritual as a natural and healthy psychological function.
The Varieties of Religious Experience has been so successful that it has been reprinted thirty-six times. It is lauded as being as influential and as significant in the twentieth century as it was when first published. To emphasize this point, the board of the Modern Library established

that James's book is the second-best nonfiction book of the twentieth century.

James, a member of the New Thought movement, influenced many and although the New Thought movement never became very large, the theories had wide general acceptance. Many NT proponents influenced Bill W. and early AA members who sought a "God of their understanding"[6].

William James

William James (January 11, 1842 – August 26, 1910)

He was the son of Henry James Sr., an independently wealthy and notoriously eccentric Swedenborgian theologian well acquainted with the literary and intellectual elites of his day.

James was influenced by Emmanuel Swedenborg, whose father first introduced him to this idea. We can only wonder how this interest influenced Bill W. as he and Lois also became interested in this religion.

James Allen

James Allen was called the unrewarded genius and a literary mystery man. This was because his inspirational writings have influenced millions. (Today, he remains an unknown author by the general public. His name is hardly even mentioned in the Library of Congress or the British Museum). Throughout his brief life, James Allen (1864-1912), sought to reside in areas of tranquility while the raging tides of change brought about by the Industrial Revolution in England raged on. The outer conditions of his world amidst these turbulent times inspired him to write a series of brilliant works that presented his personal philosophy[6].

James worked as a private secretary (administrative assistant) in 1902; he decided to devote all of his time to writing. Tragically, his literary career was quite short, lasting only 10 years. However, he amazingly wrote 19 books in that time period. These rich outpourings of thoughts and ideas have survived to inspire those in the generations that followed[6].

His most popular book, "As a Man Thinketh" has had the greatest influence on AA members than any of his others. This brief, but very powerful treatise on positive thinking, provided inspiration and strength to those early members of AA who struggled with their own demons.

Allen insisted upon the power of every individual to form his own personality and to create his own happiness. Thought and character are the same and outside conditions of a person's life will always be matched or related to his inner state. {Note: Relates to AA's Step 2 - unmanageability; fix the insides and the outside will change.} William James confirms this line of thinking when he states that most mind-cures postulate the theory that thoughts are "forces" and that if like attracts like, then one man's thought will attract to him thoughts of the same type that exist in the outer world. Thus one gets by ones thinking, a confirmation of their desire from elsewhere and the primary purpose of our lives is to engage the heavenly forces to bring forth the conditions we are seeking[6].

Stated quite simply "a man is literally what he thinks, his character being the complete sum of all his thoughts." – James Allen

Emmet Fox (1886-1951)

One of the most influential NT authors of the 20th Century was Emmett Fox He was born in Ireland on July 30, 1886, was educated in England, pursued has spiritual career in the Unites States and died in France on August 13, 1951. He was profoundly influenced by an early teacher of mental science, Thomas Troward

When Fox arrived in the United States in 1931, he was quickly selected to become the minister of New York's Church of the Healing Christ. He became immensely popular in short order and gave talks to some of the largest audiences ever assembled in New York's Hippodrome Theater and Carnegie Hall. His secretary was the mother of a new member of AA that Bill W. worked with and as a result, early New York AA members frequently went to hear him speak[12].

Fox's most famous work, "The Sermon on the Mount" was not only a suggested reading by early AA members, but became immensely popular and was the most read book in AA circles prior to the publishing of the book, "Alcoholics Anonymous". His book was frequently sold at AA meetings in the early days and on into the mid 1940's. In Akron, "as soon as men in the hospital could begin to focus their eyes, they got a copy of "Sermon on the Mount".

It is noteworthy that after the Akron AA split from the Oxford group in November of 1939, the first AA meeting held at Dr. Bob's was led by Dr. Bob and after identifying himself as an alcoholic, he began reading from "Sermon on the Mount" by Emmet Fox. This occurrence as well as the tremendous influence of Emmet Fox on AA can be found in " Dr. Bob and the Good Oldtimers"[15].

The fundamental appeal and contribution of Emmet Fox to Alcoholics Anonymous lies in the simplicity and power of "The Sermon on the Mount." This book sets forth the basic principles of the New Thought philosophy that "God is the only power, and that evil is insubstantial; that we form our own destiny by our thoughts and our beliefs; that conditions do not matter when we pray; that time and space and matter are human illusions; that there is a solution to every problem; that man is the child of God, and God is perfect good."[9]

At the core of New Thought philosophy is the idea that love and personal forgiveness are the keys to fundamental transformation: Fox states "Love is by far the most important thing of all. It is the Golden Gate of Paradise. Pray for the understanding of love, and meditate upon it daily. It casts out fear. It is the fulfilling of the Law. It covers a multitude of sins. Love is absolutely invincible."

He goes on to say that forgiveness is an integral part of the Pathway of Love, "which is open to everyone in all circumstances, and upon which you may step at any moment - at this moment if you like - requires no formal introduction, has no conditions whatever. It calls for no expensive laboratory in which to work, because your own daily life, and your ordinary daily surroundings are your laboratory. It needs no reference library, no professional training, no external apparatus of any kind. All it does need is that you should begin steadfastly to expel from your mentality every thought of personal condemnation (you must condemn a wrong action, but not the actor), of resentment for old injuries, and of everything which is contrary to the law of Love. You must not allow yourself to hate either person, or group, or nation, or anything whatever"[12].

"You must build-up by faithful daily exercise the true Love-consciousness, and then all the rest of spiritual development will follow upon that. Love will heal you. Love will illumine you."

The reader can quickly see why the writing's of Emmet Fox had such great appeal to early AA's and that appeal continues to this day. The cornerstones of Fox's philosophy is to live "one day at a time", to be responsible for your own thoughts and to promptly address resentments. Bill took note of this line of thinking and it would make its way into the Big Book.

For Fox, one of the most important rules for growth was to live in the present: "Live in today, and do not allow yourself to live in the past under any pretense. Living in the past means thinking about the past, rehearsing past events, especially if you do this with feeling...train yourself to be a man or woman who lives one day at a time. You'll be surprised how rapidly conditions will change for the better when you approach this ideal."[16]

Emmet Fox emphasized the idea that thoughts are real things, and that one cannot have one kind of mind and another kind of life. According to Fox, if we want to change our lives, then we must change our thoughts first. This idea is at the core of AA's step 2, "change the inner condition and the outer condition will follow". Many of his simply stated profundities have contributed to an AA philosophy that has transformed the lives of literally millions of recovering alcoholics

Thomas Troward (1847-1916)

Early Teacher of Mental Science

Thomas Troward was Her Majesty's Assistant Commissioner and later Divisional Judge of the North Indian Punjab from 1869 until his retirement in 1896. It is this later period for which he is best remembered and most celebrated; in it he was at last able to devote himself to his great interest in metaphysical and esoteric studies.

The most notable results were a few small volumes that have had a profound effect on the development of spiritual metaphysics, in particular that of the New Thought Movement, of which the teaching known as Science of Mind is Troward's most direct legacy. He was an influential figure in the development of Ernest Holmes' Religious Science/Science of Mind organization due to the impact his philosophy had on Holmes, and Troward's teachings are regularly taught in Science of Mind classes.

53

New Thought as a powerful influence on Bill W.

The ideas from the Christian Science and NT had a great appeal to Bill and we can only imagine what influence it had on him while he lay in Townes Hospital recovering from his last relapse. Just a few months before this he had twice read Mary Eddy Bakers, *Science and Health with Key to the Scriptures,* with the hope of strengthening his willpower which would aide him in his battle with alcohol[14].

While in confinement at Townes Hospital, Ebby Thatcher (childhood friend and sponsor to Bill W.), gave Bill W. a book that would have great impact on him. That book was William James *The Varieties of Religious Experience* and was used by Bill in Appendix II in the book "Alcoholics Anonymous" (Big Book) where he used it to clarify the terms "spiritual experience" and "spiritual awakening". He went on to say that James had determined the majority of these types of phenomena are what he called the "educational variety" because they developed slowly over a period of time[17].

Some years later, while Bill was writing the Big Book, he certainly used much material from a wide variety of sources. William James's book was one such source. James had written that certain religions worked for people when certain criteria were met. He presented the idea that no matter what it was called, it was the same process at work. For example, any person who becomes willing to change has to abandon their old behavior and adopt a new set of behaviors once committed to this new way of life, the answers come. "Surrender to win" was gleaned from this line of thinking[16].

Another hugely important idea that can be seen throughout the book *Alcoholics Anonymous* is the accessibility and availability of God or Higher Power. The Higher Power concept is taught in NT to be All Powerful, Guiding, Creative Intelligence, terms that can be found in the Big Book.

The appeal of New Thought to the founders of AA

If one were to read the writings of just a few of the more outstanding members of the NT movement, you would quickly see why they had such great acceptance and understood their appeal to the founders of AA.

Many New Thought writers were on the recommended reading book list that was suggested that the early AA members should read. The list included James Allen, "As a Man Thinketh", Thomas Troward's, "Edinburgh Lectures in Mental Health", William James, "Varieties of Religious Experiences", and Emmett Fox, "Sermon on the Mount"[16].

One main attraction for the newly sober and seeking alcoholics of early AA was that similar to the Oxford Group's program, New Thought changed religious beliefs into a daily plan of action that gave them a sense of stability and provided the ability to solve problems in the present moment.

Another appealing and useful concept that Bill would use in the eleventh step was "conscious contact". Both NT and the Oxford Group suggested "seeking guidance", this and the firm understanding of the importance of keeping one's thinking positive and removing thoughts of grievance and resentment and always maintaining an attitude of forgiveness. Both groups taught and understood that one's thinking will ultimately produce corresponding results in a person's life[18].

From the very beginning and primarily due to the influence of NT on early AA, the role of one's thinking in maintaining sobriety was a major part of a program of action. AA members openly discussed topics such as "stinkin thinkin" leading to "stinkin drinken" and the importance of having "an attitude of gratitude". The practice of taking a moral inventory and identifying those things that blocked us from source were practices that would aide in cleaning up one's thinking and thereby improve one's life.

1872

Alcoholics Anonymous and the Influence of Religion

As we can see Alcoholics Anonymous was influenced from many Social Movements as well as organized Religion, specifically Christianity, which contains the very taproots of the fellowship. The evangelically oriented religious leaders that had begun the Temperance movement in the nineteenth and twentieth centuries", in time, would establish organizations and missions for the suffering alcoholic. Many of these religious movements and their ideas would benefit and influence a series of individuals that would lead directly to Bill Wilson.

Jerry McAuley

Jerry McAuley opened the Water St. Mission in the notorious Fourth Ward of NYC. It marked the beginning of the urban mission movement. The movement, which spread across America by the Salvation Army, focused its message to the Skid Row alcoholic. Jerry contributed in several ways to ideas that would be used by early AA members. One key idea learned by Jerry, the hard way, was when he made the mistake of thinking he could drink beer with impunity. Alcoholics cannot drink alcohol in any form.

When McAuley passed away (in 1884) S. H. Hadley succeeded him. Hadley's example of recovery from alcoholism was cited in William James' book *The Varieties of Religious Experience*. Hadley's son, Harry, later collaborated with Rev Sam Shoemaker to establish a rescue mission at Calvary Episcopal Church in NYC. This mission would later serve as the base from which Ebby T. would stay as he set out to help Bill W. Jerry was one of those who proved that a religious conversion can be a method to achieve sobriety for the alcoholic[1].

Jerry McAuley

He was one of those who proved that a religious conversion can be a method to achieve sobriety for the alcoholic.

1878 General William Booth and the Salvation Army

William Booth (10 April 1829 – 20 August 1912)

A British Methodist Preacher who founded The Salvation Army and became its first General.

Booth was one of the first religious leaders to suggest alcoholism was a disease. He demonstrated an effective understanding of the disease as an uncontrollable compulsion that held the afflicted as "abject slaves of the intoxicating cup".

In his book, In *Darkest England and the Way Out,* he provided stories of alcoholics who had once been hopeless but had recovered through the Salvation Army conversion process. He noted that many of the Salvation Army workers who were once beyond human aide were now freed from bondage and helping others who were attempting to recover[2].

In 1909 a writer, Harold Begbie, made the work being done by General Booth and his Salvation Army the subject of a book *Twice-Born Men.* The book was dedicated to Professor William James. (A sequel would be written in 1923 with the Oxford Group as the subject of this second book "More Twice-Born Men". Both books were an inspiration to Frank Buchman, founder of the Oxford Group, and his work with alcoholics.)

The format of *Twice-Born Men* is thought by some to have been a source used by Bill W. when he was laying out the book "Alcoholics Anonymous". In Begbie's book he quotes William James and his teachings as written in *The Varieties of Religious Experience* as Bill does in the Big Book and Begbie's book also contains stories of alcoholics who found recovery through a religious conversion experience. This was the most important point of the book and confirmed William James and many others belief in the spiritual experience as the answer to a hopeless condition[3].

The work done by General Booth and others, long before AA was founded, proved that the conversion experience could be effective in overcoming alcoholism. When Bill Wilson began his work with alcoholics, this fact having been firmly established left him with the daunting task of developing a method that could be used by large numbers of alcoholics to create this type of experience. (Later this will be called the 12 step process)[1].

1909 - Harold Begbie – *Twice Born Men*

Edward Harold Begbie (1871–1929), also known as Harold Begbie, was an English author and journalist who published nearly 50 books and poems and contributed to periodicals.

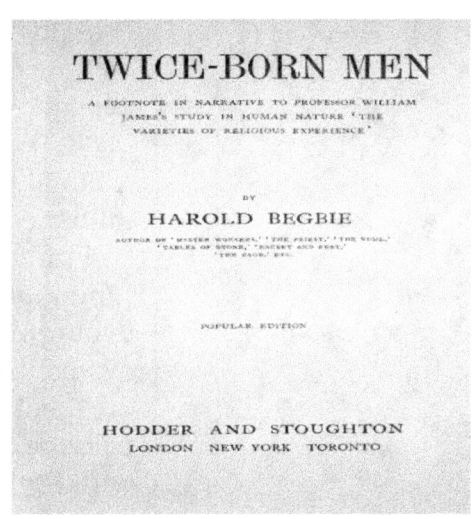

What is ' conversion '?

According to Professor James, in whose steps we follow with admiration and respect, ' to be converted, to be regenerated, to receive grace, to experience religion, to gain assurance, are so many phrases which denote the process, gradual or sudden, by which a self hitherto divided, and consciously wrong inferior and unhappy, becomes unified and consciously right superior and happy, in consequence of its firmer hold upon religious realities.'

Elsewhere he speaks of ' those striking instantaneous instances of which Saint Paul's is the most eminent, and in which often, amid tremendous emotional excitement or perturbation of the senses, a complete division is established in the twinkling of an eye between the old life and the new.'

Dwight L. Moody

Dwight L. Moody

Dwight Lyman Moody (February 5, 1837 - December 22, 1899), also known as D.L. Moody, was an American evangelist and publisher

Among the three main influences that played on Frank Buchman (Founder of the Oxford Group) was American evangelism of the early 20th century and his own personal identification with Dwight L. Moody[4].

He has been called the greatest evangelist of the last century by many and the spiritual roots he planted influenced Frank Buchman (founder of the Oxford Group) and have survived in varied forms in AA. Conferences he conducted influenced whole generations of ministers including Samuel Shoemaker, Oxford Group leader and Robert E. Speer, the originator of the Four Absolutes of the Oxford Group[1].

There is no doubt that these evangelists would be shocked and uncomfortable with the way today's AA uses their principles and dismayed at the use of higher power instead of Jesus, to say nothing of the language used at AA meetings, but they would totally be in awe of AA's success in dealing with the alcoholic.

Part 3
The Emmanuel Movement

1906

The Emmanuel Movement

The Rev. Drs. Elwood Worcester and Samuel McComb opened a clinic in the Emmanuel Church in Boston, MA. It introduced the use of spirituality in the treatment of diseases that included alcoholism along with the use of recovered alcoholics as lay therapists. Among the noted lay therapists were C. Baylor and Richard Peabody[1].

When Rev. Elwood Worcester founded the Emmanuel Movement (EM) in 1906 it was to provide an alternative to the well established Christian Science Church and the NT movements. The Episcopal Church and others were being challenged by the advancement of science especially from Darwinism and psychiatry with Sigmund Freud leading the assault[2].

Dr. Elwood Worcester

Dr Elwood Worcester (1862-1940)

An Episcopal clergyman and founder of the Emmanuel Movement which pioneered medicine and psychotherapy in conjunction with spiritual practices for the alcoholic and other nervous disorders.

The late 19th century had been a time of great theological and intellectual advances that had risen from a tremendous convergence of science, religion and thought. When first founded, the Emmanuel Movement (a name given by the press) was not to provide treatment for alcoholic and drug addicts but for the support and treatment of other maladies such as tuberculosis and a variety of "nervous" conditions. At the Emmanuel Clinic Elwood Worcester with the assistance of Dr. Samuel McComb attempted to harness the some healing powers that were being used by Christian Science. They felt that these powers were the same used by Jesus in the early Christian Church[1].

With the merging of Theology and medicine, Dr. Worcester and Dr. Mc Comb brought together for the first time both fields in the treatment of consumption (tuberculosis), nervous conditions including alcoholism. Although the number of alcoholics who received treatment at the EM clinic was never extremely large, it was the starting place where the use of group therapy (fellowship), psychology (medicine) and religion were used to treat the disease of alcoholism[1].

Worcester has been given credit as being among the first to use of psychology and religion in the field of "recovery" from diseases of the body mind and spirit. The same approach would be picked up by Bill W. in 1935 and who acknowledged the support from the fields of medicine and religion[3].

During its brief span of 23 years, the EM made tremendous advances in the treatment of the alcoholic. They helped promote the disease concept and acceptance within the medical community. This work without doubt, contributed to the foundation upon which AA was built.

One "off-shoot" of the EM was the Jacoby Club, founded in 1909. Both the EM and the Jacoby Club are noted as important predecessors to AA. The Club stressed the importance of self help and mutual aid that is, the recovered helping the unrecovered. Dr. Worcester saw the importance of fellowship among his patients and established a spiritual conversion as the only way to lasting sobriety. [4]

These two concepts were endorsed by William James and serve as early influence in the development of AA. Bill W. often said that "early AA got its ideas of self examination, acknowledgement of character defects, restitution for harm done and working with others from many sources"[7]. The EM is a good example of one "source".

In 1909 the Jacoby Club was launched by Emmanuel Church member and prominent rubber merchant Ernest Jacoby. He organized what he called "men meeting men" meetings in the church's basement. They were originally designed as informal auxiliary meetings for people who were affected by drinking problems to meet and help each other. The group grew rapidly and moved out of the Emmanuel Church in September 1913. For the next several decades it sought "down-and-out" men and put a special emphasis on fellowship as a path to recovery.

In 1940, Paddy Keegan came to Boston to start the first A.A. group in that city, and linked his Boston work with the Jacoby Club. Ruth Hock at the New York A.A. office put Boston alcoholics in contact with Lawrence Hatlestad, the man who was running the Jacoby Club's program for alcoholics.

In May 1942, that a Boston businessman named Richmond Walker came to his first A.A. meeting and got sober. Six years later, in 1948, Rich published (on his own) a little A.A. meditational book called *Twenty-Four Hours a Day*, which quickly began sweeping the country. He is the second most highly published A.A. author (only Bill W. is more widely published), and is of enormous importance to A.A. history. For many years there were probably more A.A. members who owned a copy of Rich's little black book than a copy of the Big Book itself.

Walker had been educated in the same mix of ideas there in Boston which had produced the Emmanuel Movement and the Jacoby Club, and the A.A. "old-timers" who first introduced him to the program had (most of them) started out in the Jacoby Club. So in his book, Rich stressed the same three central necessities for recovery: spirituality, "re-educating" our subconscious minds, and drawing on the healing power of fellowship among recovering alcoholics.[8]

1913
Courtney Baylor – the first Alcoholism therapist

In 1913, Courtney Baylor began to work at the Emmanuel clinic as a specialist in alcoholism. He has been given the credit as being the first lay alcoholism therapist in the United States. However, similar to Worcester, Baylor did not just treat alcoholics; he focused a large majority of his work on a variety of nervous conditions that included alcoholism. In the forward to Baylor's book, *Remaking a Man*, Worcester describes the wide range of types of patients that he had seen "come and go" from Baylor's office. He said they represented all types of educated men that came from all walks of socio-economic society...ranging from "any single rank in life". He went on to say that while many came to the clinic with alcoholism, many others sought help for: "ordinary neuroses and psychoses - depression, fear, weakness of will, painful thoughts, insomnia, evil temper, lack of mental concentration, with resultant talk of failure, impoverishment and discouragement."[1]

Baylor originally went to the Emmanuel clinic in 1911 for help with his own drinking problem and in the spirit of mutual aid (the recovered helping the unrecovered) he became a paid "friendly visitor" in the social services dept. of the Emmanuel Church. He continued this work until Dr. Worcester retired in 1929 after which they both left the church to found and work at the Craigie Foundation of Boston. In 1945 Baylor returned to the EM Church and his previous job[1].

Baylor used the Emmanuel Church's model of social service and mutual-aid in his work. He did not place a professional distance between himself and his patients. He shared the fact that he was alcoholic and he was honest and open in regards to this with his patients. He only required mutual confidentiality as a prerequisite of his treating them. This approach was unlike Richard Peabody who did not share any personal information with his patients. This unique relationship is similar to the AA sponsor or the person doing a 12th step and the principle of one alcoholic sharing with another was proven to be without parallel. Baylor's patients soon found themselves acting in a dual capacity, one as the patient and one as the physician. This fostered the patient to become responsible for the work they were engaged in and they became able to help those help themselves[1].

While a therapist at the Emmanuel Clinic during the years 1933-1934, Baylor had a patient, Rowland Hazard, who has the distinction of establishing a direct link between the EM and the formation of AA[4]. In addition, Rowland became an Oxford Group member after returning from Europe, where he had been seeing Dr. Carl Jung. This one man has the rare notoriety of being an Emmanuel Movement member and Oxford Group member[4]. It was he who had the direct contact with Bill W. in NYC at the Episcopal Church run by Sam Shoemaker[4].

In August 1934, Rowland had been working with alcoholics at the Episcopal Church and had the occasion to help another important AA member who would 12 step Bill W. on a bleak day in November, 1934...and that man was Ebby Thatcher. Rowland, Ebby and Bill attended Oxford Group meetings together[4].

This one man, Rowland had a tremendous influence on the formation of AA in 1935 and served as the messenger to the messenger that helped Bill W[4].

1919

Courtney Baylor *Remaking a Man*

Baylor's book, *Remaking a Man* which described his treatment methods, was read by Bill and early AA's. Besides his most influential patient, as far as AA is concerned, Rowland H., Baylor had another patient, Richard Peabody, who would also write a book entitled *The Common Sense of Drinking.* The personal copy of Peabody's book belonging to Bill W. is now in the AA Archives, and contains the following inscription: "Dr. Peabody was as far as is known, the first authority to state, "Once and alcoholic, always an alcoholic"[4].

1921
Richard Peabody

Peabody, a patient of Courtney Baylor was the son of a well known Boston family who went to the EM clinic for treatment of his alcoholism. Peabody attended the churches clinic and weekly health classes during 1921 and 1922. By 1924, he became a volunteer at the EM church and during this time period, he had some remarkable success in the treatment of alcoholics. In the 1930's, Peabody was publishing articles in both medical and lay literature describing his method of treating alcoholism[1].

Peabody's approach was quite different from those that had been practiced by earlier EM therapists. Where Dr. Worcester and Courtney Baylor encouraged fellowship, mutual aid, and spiritual conversion, Peabody distanced himself from his patients and did not encourage fellowship and their joining the Jacoby Club (The Jacoby Club was "the fellowship" at this time).

Having a limited education in terms of medicine or psychiatry, he had a small area in which to develop his practice in the 1920's. The dilemma he faced was that he did not want to imitate the methods used by psychiatrists and could not, based on his lack of credentials, work as an M.D. He also did not wish to be viewed as an Evangelical Church Therapist like Worcester and most definitely did not want to be seen as a "feather-decorated, painted medicine man". What he used to justify his position and the exorbitant fees he charged was that his method of lay therapy could speed up the recovery process.[1]

He had promised in his book to avoid moralizing, and had written about presenting a strictly scientific approach. Peabody used psychotherapy almost exclusively and possessed the fatal assumption of excluding spirituality from his treatment. In addition, he did not acknowledge that alcoholics had guilt and shame and as a result had no mechanism by which forgiveness and restitution could be attained. (In AA terms, he had no 9th step in place to deal with these troublesome features of early sobriety.)

THE EMMAUEL MOVEMENT

REMAKING A MAN

One Successful Method of Mental Refitting

By Courtenay Baylor

OF THE EMMANUEL MOVEMENT, Boston, 1919

FORWARD to *Remaking a Man* by Elwood Worcester

The writer's one object in his psychological work has been to obtain results. He has therefore explained his ideas to his patients in the language each individual would understand. Since his experience has been that of a layman talking entirely to laymen, he has not acquired a technical vocabulary. This he regrets as he is perfectly conscious of the value of technical terminology in arriving at an exact expression of one's ideas when addressing scientific men. He asks, therefore, that those readers to whom his terminology may seem crude will criticize his methods and results rather than the terms he uses to describe them in this paper[5].

"Getting the man to stop drinking is only the first step in a very long march. All the negative traits induced by alcohol must be eliminated and the positive traits put in their places. Irritability, self-pity, fear, worry, criticism of friends, bitter hatred of enemies, lack of concentration, lack of initiative and action, all these must be worked out of the character. The entire mental process must be changed, a new sense must be grown, one that can recognize the soul; when this is accomplished we have the man himself cured from alcoholism." Courtney Baylor[5]

One of Peabody's main approaches was to appeal to the alcoholic's ego by instilling the idea that they would not want to appear stupid. Nobody wants to look bad was the basis for this line of thinking.

A curious feature of his method was that he made no attempt to take care of the moralizing aspect of his method, by calling the alcoholism a malady or a disease. Using the disease concept would have been readily accepted and had been in use from the time of Dr. Benjamin Rush and his description of habitual drunkenness as a "progressive and odious disease". In addition, he could have easily used the word "alcoholism" as it was introduced by Dr. Magnus Huss in 1849.

Several reasons for his reluctance to present his method for the treatment of a disease process is that he had no credentials and he did not use his own experience as an alcoholic for his claim of providing a strictly "scientific approach" for the malady. His underlying belief system was that a disease had a connection to the body and this was tied to the "mind-cure" movement, including Christian Science, which he wanted to avoid[1].

Peabody continued to use several important ideas he had learned from Baylor: surrender, relaxation, suggestion and catharsis. His development and reformulation of some of these, particularly surrender and suggestion, was much more specific to and useful for an alcoholic's particular situation than the formulations of Worcester and Baylor.

Peabody was very clear about the new priorities for a reordered life. "The first step to sobriety is surrender to the fact that the alcoholic cannot drink again without bringing disastrous results" and "this surrender is the absolute starting point. The conviction of its supreme importance is an absolute necessity. With surrender, halfway measures are of no avail." (This was undoubtedly the source of Bill Wilson's better known phrase: "Half measures avail us nothing.")[8]

{Note: Bill W. and Richard Peabody served in the same artillery training camp in Plattsburg, NY in May of 1917. Though they were not destined to meet until later, this is an interesting synchronicity.}

By the 1930's the Emmanuel Movement had all but been forgotten

The Emmanuel Movement had been limited to a small geographic area and a rather small number of alcoholics were reached. The core of the movement consisted of three major individuals (Worcester, Baylor and Peabody), each with their own theory of treatment and agenda. During the time span from 1906 to the mid 1930's three distinct phases emerged with varying degrees of success. The major significance the EM's work was the hope that it gave, both to the researchers in the early scientific study of alcoholism and that alcoholism was a treatable condition[1].

The movement was self limiting in that as each of the founding members moved on or as in the case of Peabody relapsed, the movement had no organization in place to continue the work. From this experience Bill Wilson would come to realize that if AA was to carry on after his passing, then there had to be a plan in place for the survival of Alcoholics Anonymous.

There are many other things Bill Wilson would learn from the Emmanuel Movement. The books written by Baylor and Peabody served as reference sources and it is very clear that Bill used them in the writing of *Alcoholics Anonymous* as he uses certain wording and phases almost verbatim.

In addition it was fellowship between recovering people that was a vital part of the approach which the Emmanuel Movement and the Jacoby Club used that Bill would observe and use in the fellowship of AA[4].

The Emmanuel approach deserved its reputation for therapeutic success in the treatment of alcoholics; however, from the point of view of recovery, far more has been accomplished in the past 50 years by those who appreciated Worcester's paradox that "the unmanageability of life may be turned around by relaxing control, not by more frenzied efforts to regain it"[1]

Part 4 – The Oxford Group and Alcoholics Anonymous

The Oxford Group and Alcoholics Anonymous

There exists an amazing series of synchronistic events that took place between the years 1908 and 1935. The sequence of events that unfolded during this time period made it possible for the meeting in Akron, Ohio between AA Co-founders, Dr. Robert Holcomb Smith and William Griffith Wilson. The timing and placement of these two individuals at the precise time and location resulted in the subsequent birth of Alcoholics Anonymous. The meeting was held at the home of Henrietta Seiberling in May 1935 and as fate would have it was the climax of the final and monumental "founding moment"[7] of a spiritual movement that would transform the lives of countless suffering alcoholics and would make Bill W. a household name.

The list of people who contributed to making possible the historic and fortuitous meeting of two alcoholics (Bill W. and Dr. Bob), befriended by the Oxford Group and who had arrived at their respective turning points simultaneously, includes: Carl Jung, Jim Newton, Harvey and Russell Firestone, Frank Buchman, Rev. Samuel Shoemaker, Rowland Hazard, Sheppard Cornell, Cebra Graves, Ebby Thatcher, Henrietta Seiberling, Rev. Walter Tunks, and T. Henry and Clarace Williams[2]. If it were not for these people who were at a point in their own lives that placed them in a position to act out their roles as key links in the chain of events that culminated in the meeting between our two main players; perhaps the fellowship to which many owe their lives today might never have been born.[2]

We will trace the lives and histories of several individuals in the cast of characters who played an integral part in every twist and turn in the Path to Fellowship and the very path that led Bill Wilson to Akron, Ohio. As we trace the paths of the players the reader will experience an astonishing series of critical events that took place in such a miraculous way.

Let us begin with the first of the "four founding moments"[6] of Alcoholics Anonymous and then proceed to examine the Oxford Group and its founder Frank Buchman. During the telling of the story we will identify and discuss each of the founding moments and discover that a golden thread of synchronistic events runs through each and terminates in Akron, Ohio the birthplace of AA[7].

Dr. Carl Jung's conversation with Rowland Hazard

In Alcoholics Anonymous, the tradition of storytelling is a prominent part of the program. The Big Book contains many stories that speak to both the inevitability of pain and the possibility of healing within the pain. The rest of the book is dedicated to the stories of members and how they recovered from their malady. They believed their drinking to be hopeless but were able to find hope as seen in their personal stories. Through storytelling they develop a message of hope and a way of passing on that hope. This process leads them on the path to a new way of life and they discover that this new way of life can be learned as well as taught by sharing their story in a general way what they used to be like, what happened, and what they are like now.[6]

Rowland Hazard

He has been immortalized in AA legend as the "certain American business man" on page 26 in the Big Book of Alcoholics Anonymous. It goes on to say;" he had ability, good sense, and high character. For years he had floundered from one sanitarium to another. He had consulted the best known American psychiatrists. Then he had gone to Europe, placing himself in the care of a celebrated physician (the psychiatrist, Dr. Jung) who prescribed for him"[3.]

We know from family records that Rowland was treated by Dr. Jung in 1931; however, recent discoveries bring into question the exact timing of his treatment period. Whatever the exact time was, the important point for our story is that it was from Dr. Jung that Rowland received the verdict that the only a spiritual conversion experience could save him[16].

Rowland Hazard III was born in Peace Dale, Rhode Island, on October 29, 1881. Rowland ("Roy") represented the tenth generation of his family in Rhode Island. The first American Hazard, Thomas, was born in 1610; he came over to the New World after the British had begun settling in Massachusetts, taking up his residence first in Boston, then the Massachusetts Bay Colony. Roy was the eldest of five children born to woolen manufacturer Rowland Gibson Hazard and Mary Pierrepont Bushnell. Hazard graduated from the Taft School in Waterbury, Connecticut, and Yale University (1903) with a B.A. degree. His prominent family standing no doubt placed him in a position to be seen by one of the worlds most famous and sought after doctors (Carl Jung) [10]

At some point He had become an alcoholic, requiring hospitalization on more than one occasion as is reported in the Big Book reference of his "floundering from one sanitarium to another"[3]. In the traditional A.A. version, it is said that he had been unable to stop relapsing in spite of extensive Jungian therapy, until finally Jung told him that with alcoholics of his type only a spiritual conversion of some sort, would enable him to radically remake and remold his inner spirit and this would give him freedom from his overwhelming compulsion to drink.

An examination of the well documented correspondence between Bill Wilson and Dr. Jung clearly demonstrates just how vitally important to the founding of Alcoholics Anonymous was this one conversation and places Rowland Hazard in the position of great significance in terms of the role he played. We will see during further examination that Rowland stands alone as perhaps the one and only person that had great influence on two of the founding moments of the fellowship of AA.

In a letter to Dr. Jung, dated January 23, 1961, Bill W. wrote one of the most eloquent letters he had ever penned. Bill wrote: "I doubt if you are aware that a certain conversation you had with one of your patients, a Mr. Roland H- in the early 1930's, did play a critical role in the founding of our fellowship"[4].

Bill goes on in his letter to say:

"Having exhausted other means of recovery from his alcoholism, it was about 1931 that he became your patient. I believe he remained under your care for perhaps a year. His admiration for you was boundless, and he left you with a feeling of much confidence."[4]

"To his great consternation, he soon relapsed into intoxication. Certain that you were his 'Court of last resort', he again returned to your care. Then came the conversation with you that was to become the first link in the chain of events that led to the founding of Alcoholics Anonymous."

"...First of all, you frankly told him of his hopelessness, so far as any medical or psychiatric treatment might be concerned. This candid and humble statement of yours was beyond doubt the first foundation stone upon which our Society has since been built"[4].

"Coming from you, one he so trusted and admired the impact upon him was immense".

"When he then asked you if there was any hope, you told him that there might be, provided the subject of a spiritual experience- in short, a genuine conversion. You pointed out how such an experience, if brought about, might remotivate him when nothing else could. But you did caution, though, that while such experiences had sometimes brought about recovery to alcoholics, they were, nevertheless, comparatively rare. You recommended that he place himself in a religious atmosphere and hope for the best. This I believe was the substance of your advice."

"Shortly thereafter, Mr. H—joined the Oxford Group, an evangelical movement then at the height of their success in Europe, and one with which you are doubtless familiar. You will remember their large emphasis upon the principles of self-survey, confession, restitution, and the giving of one's self in the service of others. They strongly stressed meditation and prayer. In these surroundings, Roland H.-did find a conversion experience that released him for the time being from his compulsion to drink".[3]

In the letter Bill went on to describe his own spiritual awakening, the subsequent founding of AA, and the spiritual experiences of its many thousands of members. As Bill wrote: "This concept proved to be the foundation of such success as Alcoholics Anonymous has since achieved. This has made the conversion experience...available on an almost wholesale basis."[4]

The closing of this letter was absolutely most gracious and profound:

"... As you will now clearly see, this astonishing chain of events actually started long ago in your consulting room, and it was directly founded on your own humility and deep perception."

The Birth of an Idea

Ideas and thoughts have an origin and path that they travel during their development and can be traced to a specific point in time. The idea that such a conversion experience could be used in the treatment of alcoholism had its beginning with the conversation between Dr. Jung and Rowland Hazard as far as AA legend is concerned and as we know this idea would later be used by Bill W. and Dr. Bob as they developed the program and fellowship of Alcoholics Anonymous.[7]

As the story continues, after leaving the care of Dr. Jung, Rowland returned to New York City, he joined and became very active in the Oxford Group and began working with other alcoholics at the United States headquarters that was located in the Calvary Episcopal Church of Rev. Samuel Shoemaker.

Although the focus of the Oxford Group did not lie solely in helping alcoholics to recover, Rowland chose to devote to sufferers of the malady his efforts and through this work he discovered a way of experiencing his own spiritual awakening. The fact that he had his conversion experience as the result of working with others, Rowland became the first in line at the gateway that led down the Path to the fellowship of Alcoholics Anonymous. He set the first cornerstone upon which the spiritual structure of AA was built and that was one alcoholic working with another*. Thus, with miraculous results,* the recovered helping the unrecovered, became the primary source for AA's fifth tradition; our primary purpose is to stay sober and help another alcoholic to achieve sobriety[16].

Rowland is also well-known in A.A. legend as one of the Oxford Group who rescued Ebby Thatcher and got him sober when Ebby was threatened with commitment to six months in Windsor Prison in August 1934. Rowland, who had made a project out of sobering Ebby, took two fellow Oxford Groupers with him, Sheppard Cornell and Cebra Graves. Both had done considerable drinking with Ebby. It was in the court of Cebra's father Judge Graves that the Ebby was released into their custody[16].

Rowland passes on what was given to him by the Oxford Group

Rowland had introduced Ebby to the four principles of the Oxford Group: absolute honesty, absolute purity, absolute unselfishness, and absolute love. "He was particularly strong in advocating absolute honesty," Ebby said "Honesty with yourself, honesty with your fellow man, honesty with God. And these things he followed himself, and thereby, by example, he made me believe in them again as I had as a young man."[14]

After his scrape with the law, with Rowland's help, Ebby closed up the family house in Manchester. For a short time he stayed at Rowland's home in Shaftsbury and then went to New York City to live at the Calvary Episcopal Mission on 23rd street. During his stay at the mission Ebby experienced profound changes in his life and his belief system. Through the guidance he was given by Rowland, Rev. Shoemaker and other's he was able to get honest about himself and his defects of character. He began making restitution were it was owed and he practiced perhaps for the first time giving without the thought of return for himself. Ebby started praying and found to his surprise that the results were immediate. He not only was released from his compulsion to drink, he also found peace of mind and a return of happiness that he had not had for years[7].

Another Factor concerning Rowland

There was another factor involved in Rowland's story, that has not been reported in accounts of his role in AA history and that is, during 1933 and that especially crucial year 1934, he was also a patient of the

Emmanuel Movement therapist Courtenay Baylor. Family records make it is clear that A.A. was influenced by the Emmanuel Movement from at least two different sources. It is commonly known that Bill W. read Richard R. Peabody's *The Common Sense of Drinking*, (a signed copy is retained in GSO archives).In addition, Bill was also in secondhand contact (via Ebby) with Rowland Hazard and hence the ideas of Courtenay Baylor, who taught something much closer to the original spiritually based Emmanuel therapy that was taught by the Rev. Elwood Worcester, who founded his clinic in 1906.[16]

The discovery that Rowland was intimately involved with Courtenay Baylor as his therapist and learned the Emmanuel tradition, in addition to his Oxford Group activities, was only made quite recently. (This fact was discovered by way of cancelled checks found in Rowland's family archives),This newly acquired information only serves to enhance the mystery of a man who played such a pivotal role in AA history and who without we may well not have the fellowship that so many literally owe their lives to.[16]

Rowland Hazard III most certainly stands alone as the only person in AA history who was both an Oxford Group member and an Emmanuel Movement participant who did so much to found the fellowship of AA and one who sadly never embraced the program to become a member. Looked at from Rowland's point of view he had no compelling reason to join AA. After all, by the time the "Big Book" was published in 1939 he had been sober eight years. His sobriety is evidenced on page 26, "Big Book"; "But this man still lives and is a free man. He does not need a bodyguard nor is he confined. He can go anywhere on this earth where other free men may go without disaster, provided he remained willing to maintain a certain simple attitude."[3]

The absence of comment by Bill, Lois, Ebby and other early A.A. members about Rowland joining AA would lead us to conclude he didn't. Lois writes in "Lois Remembers", "...he remained an ardent Oxford Grouper until his death in 1945." To the end Rowland continued his spiritual journey that had its beginnings in the consulting room of Dr. Jung; no later vicissitude had the power to shake it[17].

Ebby visits Bill Wilson at 183 Clinton Street, Brooklyn, NY

It was while staying at the mission and working with the Oxford Group that he heard of Bill's desperate situation. Shortly after the news about his childhood friend, Ebby made arrangements to visit Bill. On a dismal frost chilled day in late November 1934, Ebby found himself sitting "kitty-corner" at the kitchen table of a brownstone house that had been given to them by Dr. Clark Burnham, Lois's father. The house was cold and in shabby condition, it had clearly seen better days, the fetid odor from the occupant Bill Wilson wrecked with the smell of stale alcohol that was emitted from his breath and pores[7].

It was at this meeting between Ebby and Bill that the second founding moment of Alcoholics Anonymous had arrived[7]. During the meeting Bill who had fetched a bottle of gin form its hiding place in the overhead tank of the toilet had offered his guest a drink that was promptly refused. Bill surprised that his old drinking buddy would refuse his offering quickly asked what was up. Ebby announced to Bills surprise that he had found religion and that was how he had been able to stop drinking.

This famous scene is memorialized in Bills story in chapter 1 of the Big Book. Bill honestly questioned if Ebby's alcoholic insanity had become religious insanity. Bill listened intently as Ebby talked about all the changes that that he had experienced with the Oxford Group and how he, who was completely hopeless, had found hope by practicing the precepts of the Oxford Group.

This rather bleak and depressing scene would have a profound significance in the annals of AA history for this moment signified the birth of a second idea upon which the fellowship of AA would be built and that was the idea that; "In the kinship of common suffering, one alcoholic had been talking with another"[7].

This Spiritual principle would later find its way into the Big Book, Chapter 2 page 18;

"Highly competent psychiatrists who have dealt with us have found it sometimes impossible to persuade an alcoholic to discuss his situation without reserve. Strangely enough, wives, parents and intimate friends usually find us even more unapproachable than do the psychiatrist and the doctor. *But the ex-problem drinker who has found this solution, who is properly armed with facts about himself, can generally win the entire confidence of another alcoholic in a few hours. Until such an understanding is reached, little or nothing can be accomplished.* That the man who is making the approach has had the same difficulty, that he obviously knows what he is talking about, that his whole deportment shouts at the new prospect that he is a man with a real answer, that he has no attitude of Holier Than Thou, nothing whatever except the sincere desire to be helpful; that there are no fees to pay, no axes to grind, no people to please, no lectures to be endured—these are the conditions we have found most effective. After such an approach many take up their beds and walk again."[3]

The results of Ebby's visit

What happened on this bleak and dark November afternoon was that a seed was firmly planted in Bills alcohol drenched brain that would later develop into the core of AA. The birth of this one idea would, in time, evolve into a life saving practice for over one million people. It was the understanding that mutuality in relationships involves the spiritual axiom that; it is by giving that we receive and we receive by giving. It is in practicing this, that we recognize that we truly gain from what we seek to give, and that we are only able to give that which we already have[7].

Another concept that would be laid at Bill Wilson's feet that day was a new concept of God. Bill had been alienated from the church for a very long time and could not tolerate being preached at. However, born of his desperation and despair Bill became open-minded. Ebby explained certain things about the Oxford Group; its being non-denominational and the importance of a self searching, taking, of one's own inventory. Confession and a willingness to make restitution, and perhaps the most revolutionary idea he heard that day, was the idea of one choosing one's own concept of "God".

Bill heard Ebby describe his personal concept of God as "another power" or a "higher power". Bill Listened with great interest but deep in his heart he knew that he couldn't accept as Ebby had done, this "getting religion". This one fact would haunt Bills alcohol soaked mind for the next few days[7].

After a few days went by Ebby returned again, this time he brought a friend from the Oxford Group, Shep C. For the next few hours they both talked incessantly of ideas that seemed foreign to Bill, for he heard them share about serenity and of this he knew little. They spoke of their new life and the thrill of having obtained a sense of purpose, they talked about prayer and meditation and the love they found in being of service. When they finally departed, Bill, who had been making himself stronger and stronger drinks to brace himself against the onslaught of their ranting, became ill and immersed himself into the internal struggle that followed the next day...

Ebby was the messenger to Bill W. of his victory over alcohol through a spiritual way of life. But even if Ebby was the one who actually talked with Bill, Rowland is recognized in the A.A. tradition as "the messenger behind the messenger,"[16]

Emerging Events set the stage

In the ten year period before the founding of AA a series of events played out in perfect order. We see how, through the machinery of the Oxford Group and its key leaders, Frank Buchman and Sam Shoemaker, events unfolded to make possible this meeting between Bob and Bill in Akron in 1935[2].

Shep, Cebra, and Rowland were all three Oxford Group members. They were part of the business teams which were working around the country in various cities. In August of 1934, Ebby surrendered his life to God at the Calvary Episcopal Church mission run by Sam Shoemaker.

After the visits made by Ebby, Bill continued to drink and remained in a depressed and confused state of mind. He went over and over the conversation with Ebby and saw the value in much of what he said. He admitted to himself, that an inventory was a good idea even if honesty would prove to be difficult. But it was with Ebby's talk about God and religion that went against everything Bill believed. Bill remembered the experience he had at Winchester Cathedral and its moment of great spiritual intensity; however, it was not sufficient enough to allow him to accept what was taught by religion[7].

One undeniable truth that continued to haunt Bill was that Ebby was sober while he remained drunk. This one fact would motivate Bill to seek the answer to the question of how it was that Ebby had been able to stay sober using Oxford Group principles.

One afternoon in late December, Bill decided he could not rest until he found out for himself the secret to Ebby's victory over alcohol. He then proceeded on a journey from Brooklyn into lower midtown Manhattan via the subway. On his way, he passed a number of bars that he simply could not pass without stopping in. It was at one of these that he met a "Finn", Alec, who he brought with him to the mission on 23rd street[7].

With his new friend in tow, Bill arrived at the mission. It was during this visit that Bill made an embarrassing scene. When he approached the alter to make what drunks sneeringly refer to, "making a nose dive", he got a wild idea during the penitents march to make his surrender and give his testimonial.

Afterward Bill could never remember what he had said but he had said it in earnest and people seemed to pay attention. Bill later said "Ebby, who had been scared to death, told me with relief that I had done all right and given my life to God".

Others remembered this incident quite differently but no matter what precisely transpired it resulted in Bill's return to Towns Hospital to be detoxed one last time by Dr. William D. Silkworth.

During his return trip to the hospital he purchased what would in the end be his last drink for the rest of his life.

Bill's last trip to Townes Hospital

While at Towns Hospital and under the care of Dr. Silkworth Bill had his "white light" spiritual experience. This was the third founding moment of Alcoholics Anonymous. After leaving the hospital, Bill immediately made a decision to become very active in Oxford Group work, and to try to bring other alcoholics from Towns to the group. He visited the mission and attended Oxford Group meetings daily for the next four or five months. This he did right up to the time of the Akron trip. Not one of the drunks he brought to the mission stayed sober.

THE OXFORD GROUP

Defined by Ernest Kurtz in his Book "Not-God", "The Oxford Group was a non-denominational, theologically conservative, evangelically styled attempt to recapture the impetus and spirit of what its members understood to be primitive Christianity. It began under the name "The first century Christian Fellowship" in 1908.Its popularity under the name "Oxford Group" peaked in the late twenties and early thirties"[7].

It was founded by an American Lutheran pastor, Dr. Frank Buchman. Three profound influences that played upon Frank Buchman were his conservative Lutheran upbringing, the more traditional Protestant Evangelism which shaped a life-long interest in the process of conversion; and American evangelism of the early 20th century which traced directly to his own personal identification with Dwight L. Moody[7] (**Dwight Lyman Moody** (February 5, 1837 - December 22, 1899), also known as D.L. Moody, was an American evangelist)

In July of 1908 Buchman arrived in England to attend the Keswick Convention of evangelicals. After hearing a sermon by a woman evangelist, Jessie Penn-Lewis, he claimed a conversion experience and later helped another attendee to go through the same experience. His experiences became the key to the rest of his life's work. Returning to the US, he started his "laboratory years" where he worked out the principles he would later apply on a global scale[15].

In 1917, Sam Shoemaker had been sent to China to start a branch of the YMCA and to teach at the Princeton-in-China Program. There, in 1918, he first met Frank Buchman who told him of the four absolutes, honesty, purity, unselfishness and love. Later, Shoemaker would speak of the meeting as a major influence for the start of his ministry, that being the time when he decided to let go of self and let God guide his life[13].

The profoundly significant meeting of Frank Buchman and Sam Shoemaker in Peking (now Beijing) China in January 1918, would later prove to be extremely important not only to the founding of Alcoholics

Anonymous but also in the development of what would evolve into the Twelve Step process itself.

The Oxford Group and their principles were carried to the United States so that in both New York City and Akron, Ohio an Oxford Group was in place and functioning when Bill Wilson and Dr. Bob Smith hit their respective bottoms. These two groups would befriend and teach their principles to our co-founders before they ever met. In fact Dr. Bob had been attending Oxford Group house meetings 2 ½ years before he met Bill. Bill himself had   begun attending meetings 5 months before meeting Dr. Bob[2].

It can be said AA began under Sam's inspiration as meetings were held every Tuesday night in the Great Hall of Calvary House during late 1934 and early 1935. These Oxford Group meetings were the starting place were Bill W. and his "alcoholic squadron" first began the practice of sharing their experience, strength and hope.

Bill always heaped praise on Rev. Shoemaker and had tremendous admiration for him, to the point of calling him a Co-founder of AA on many occasions. He accredited the Oxford Group meetings at the Calvary Church and Sam as instrumental in assisting him with the writing of the "Big Book." Bill acknowledged this linkage when he wrote on page 39 of *A.A. Comes of Age*: "The early A.A. got its ideas of self-examination, acknowledgment of character defects, restitution for harm done, and working with others straight from the Oxford Groups and directly from Sam Shoemaker, their former leader in America, and from nowhere else."[8]

 It was from these early meetings that we can trace the very roots of the "word of mouth" AA program that would develop over the next four years until it was immortalized in the book, *Alcoholics Anonymous*. This, as a yet developed program that Bill and these Oxford Group members began to practice, would later be the source of Frank Amos's report to John D. Rockefeller in 1938.

This is what he had to say about the "self styled Alcoholic group of Akron, Ohio." Mr. Amos reported that the group all followed a similar technique and used the same system[18].

He described the "Program" in the following:

1. An alcoholic must realize that he is an alcoholic, incurable from a medical standpoint, and that he must never again drink anything with alcohol in it.
2. He must surrender himself absolutely to God, realizing that in himself there is no hope.
3. Not only must he want to stop drinking permanently, he must remove from his life other sins such as hatred, adultery, and others that frequently accompany alcoholism. Unless he will do this absolutely, Dr Bob and his associates refuse to work with him.
4. He must have devotions every morning-a "quiet time "of prayer and some reading from the Bible and other religious literature.
5. He must be willing to help other alcoholics get straightened out. This throws up a protective barrier and strengthens his own willpower and convictions.
6. It is important, but not vital, that he meet frequently with other reformed alcoholics and form both a social and religious comradeship.
7. Important but not vital, that he attend some religious service at least once weekly.

The earliest glimpses of Alcoholics Anonymous come into view

Immediately after his release from Towns Hospital in December 1934, Bill returned to the Oxford Group headquarters in Calvary Episcopal Church run by the Rev. Samuel Shoemaker. This was during A.A.'s formative years. It was under the guidance of Sam that Bill would begin a lifelong mission of working with others to save himself.

In later years Bill Wilson showered praise on the Reverend Sam Shoemaker. This was because in Bills earliest days, Sam, had encouraged Bill in his work with other suffering alcoholics. On one occasion Bill had received a letter from the Reverend, commending his work with an alcoholic chemistry professor. He corresponded with Rev. Shoemaker for many years and this added to the closeness of their relationship. It was in the office of Rev. Shoemaker that Bill spent hours reading the extensive library at his disposal. They had many talks during which they would discuss topics of a spiritual nature.

Wilson interacted with many of the key individuals within Sam's inner circle. The Oxford Group business team that worked out of the church included many influential men such as Rowland Hazard, Shep Cornell, Hanford Twitchell and Ebby Thatcher. This was documented in the personal diary of Rev. Shoemaker during this period of time.

Several years later while Bill was writing the book *Alcoholics Anonymous*, he asked Sam to write the twelve steps, Sam politely declined as he thought it would be best if this was left up to Bill. However, Sam did have significant influence on the writing of the Big Book and gave Bill many ideas and was a tremendous resource during the writing process[11].

Bill and the rest of the alcoholic contingent of the Oxford Group began gathering at Stewart's Cafeteria in New York following their regular meeting in early 1935. Much like meetings today this was the "meeting after the meeting". Fellowship became a large part of the early program. At these gatherings you might expect to see Rowland H., Ebby T., Shep C., Cebra G., and Bill W., as well as the newcomers that flowed through the mission[11].

Lois Wilson talked of regular attendance at the Oxford Group meetings with Bill, Shep, and Ebby. James Houck, a nonalcoholic Oxford Group member in Frederick, Maryland, stated that Bill W. went to many Oxford Group meetings at the Francis Scott Key Hotel in Frederick and the meetings always centered on alcohol. "He was obsessed with the idea of carrying the message". The conclusion is that Bill had a wide acquaintance in Oxford Group circles, not just confined to Sam and

Calvary Mission. Bill told Houck that he worked on 50 drunks in the first 6 months with no success[17].

Calvary Mission was at another location in the "gas house" district. Thousands of people passed through the mission where they offered lodging, free meals, and Oxford Group meetings every night. Tex Francisco was its superintendent in 1934 when Bill showed up there. It was from this mission that Bill would meet new members, and at some point, started taking them to live at his home on 182 Clinton Street in Brooklyn.

Critical Events lead up to an Oxford Group meeting in Akron

At this point we need to examine the set of circumstances that led to Akron as the site for an Oxford Group meeting. The choice for Akron and the events that followed the meeting would prepare the Akron cast for their part in the story. The one person who had the most influence on the choice of cities now comes into view.

The man most certainly responsible for the historic Akron meeting between Bill and Dr. Bob was Jim Newton. He was surely the sole guide that determined the Oxford Group would be in place in Akron, Ohio when Bill showed up there in May1935[2].

This amazing series of circumstances began in the early 1920's when as a young man Jim Newton "accidently" stumbled into an Oxford Group party...

Jim Newton, a luggage salesman from New York, had come upon an Oxford Group meeting quite by accident while traveling in the New England area. While out with some friends looking for a good time one night, they made their way into the meeting and became very touched by the group and were inspired to join them as members[2].

It was at this Oxford house party that he would become a lifelong member of a group that would change the course of his life. He made the decision to give his life to the direction of God and experienced a spiritual conversion with great influence from a lady, Eleanor Forde, who he would marry some twenty years later.

Jim Newton went to Ft. Myers, Florida in 1926, to visit his father. During this trip he and his father purchased a 35 acre tract of land across the road from the Thomas Edison estate. Jim became very close to Mr. and Mrs. Edison, and often acted as host and toastmaster at Edison's famous birthday parties which were attended by Henry Ford, Harvey Firestone, many world renowned business leaders and public figures.

It was at one of these parties that he would meet Harvey Firestone Sr. who later offered Jim a job as secretary to the Firestone Tire and Rubber Company in 1926, and moved him to Akron, Ohio putting him in residence at the Portage Country Club adjacent to the Firestone Estate.

When Jim first arrived in Akron he was welcomed into the Firestone family, and became close friends with the elder Firestones son, Russell Firestone known in the family as Bud. Bud had a very bad drinking problem and had already been sent to several hospitals to treat his serious condition.

Jim accompanied Bud to a Rehabilitation Facility, located on the Hudson River in New York, and stayed with him through the entire program. Then he took Bud to an Episcopal Conference in Denver where Oxford Group people had been invited. On the train heading east he was able to introduce Bud to his old Oxford Group minister, Sam Shoemaker. Alone with Sam, Bud surrendered his life to God in a private car on the train. His life changed, and his family situation and marriage were saved.

Jim worked for Firestone for eleven years and was being groomed for president of the company, when he made the decision to resign to allow him to work full time with the Oxford Groups. Firestone's clergyman was Rev. Walter Tunks. Jim joined Tunks' church and became active in fund raising efforts.

While on a trip to New York to watch the Dempsey/Tunney fight, Jim met with Frank Buchman. His life was in turmoil at this time and he wanted to make changes in the way things were going. Buchman sent Jim to the Calvary Church to meet with Sam Shoemaker who would persuade him to join the business team that Rowland Hazard and others were a part of[2].

The business teams consisted of groups of important men who made attempts to convert others to the Oxford Group method of spirituality. Jim frequently met with the aforementioned Shep Cornell and Rowland Hazard to make plans for group events.

When Jim returned to Akron to complete his business with Firestone Rubber he began attending Oxford Group meetings at the Rev. Walter Tunks Church. At these meetings he met T. Henry and Clarace Williams, husband and wife Oxford Group members. They were deeply religious people who were committed to being of service to others. In time, they would become strong supporters of the early Akron AA movement. Although not alcoholic themselves, they had compassion and sympathy for those afflicted with the disease of alcoholism.

The business team put on house parties in various cities at the finest hotels and clubs. In January of 1933, Frank Buchman, leading a team of thirty men and women, descended on Akron for the first time to give testimonials at the Mayflower Hotel and in Akron churches. They began to introduce the townspeople to the ways of the Oxford Group.

Had Jim not already been a business team member and in place in Akron, it is very unlikely that Buchman would ever have chosen this small, rather unknown city as a place to pursue his evangelistic efforts. Jim was the spokesman who introduced Buchman at all the affairs that week in Akron. Here we can clearly see that input from Jim Newton's Oxford house parties with Firestone and Tunks' Episcopal Church group influenced the choice of Akron as the site of this endeavor, rather than some other city[2].

The characters take their final places

The cast of characters is nearly complete and in place. Still to appear on the scene, however, are Henrietta Seiberling, Anne and Bob Smith.

About this time, a lady named Henrietta Seiberling, the wife of John Seiberling of the Seiberling Tire and Rubber Company, found herself with personal and marital problems, and separated from her husband. She turned to the Oxford Group and attended the first meetings held at the Mayflower Hotel. She went with a woman named Anne Smith, the wife of a well-known Akron surgeon who was in deep trouble with his drinking[7].

Two of the curious synchronicities that existed are that Bill had met Henrietta's father-in-law back in New York while doing business on Wall Street a few years earlier. He also met T. Henry Williams in the course of the proxy fight that brought Bill to Akron in the first place. Both had no idea that both were Oxford Group members at the time of their meetings and could not have envisioned the long and rich relationship they would have.

The kind and compassionate couple, T Henry and Clarace Williams, who had been impressed with the Oxford Group message, had a home to offer for a meeting place. This is the same home that several years later would be the site where the first meetings that Dr. Bob and Bill would attend were held.

A gifted and compassionate lady, Henrietta Seiberling, mastered some of the Oxford Group principles, and was using the biblical principles to help her good friend, Dr. Bob Smith, with his drinking problem. His wife, Anne, joined the effort and assembled books and spiritual readings and principles from the Bible, the Oxford Group, and various other Christian writings. They began seeking guidance and prayed for a solution to her husband's seemingly hopeless drinking problem. The talented and very alcoholic surgeon, Dr. Bob, became the focus of all these efforts. He did a lot of spiritual reading, attended a lot of meetings, but remained drunk[14].

Now all the synchronistic events converge

At this point in our story the facts merge into the story as it is presented in AA literature. Onto this scene emerges Bill Wilson from New York City.

While Bill was working with alcoholics down at the mission in NYC, he was also trying to restore his standing in Wall Street that had been totally destroyed by his drinking. But one old friend, Howard Tompkins was impressed by Bills recovery and the work he was doing. In December 1934 he sent Bill an encouraging letter that served to build his old confidence[7].

His connection with Tomkins proved to be the source of a lead that started a chain of events that began Bill's trip to Akron. Bill had heard about a proxy fight for control of a small company in Akron. Ohio. He researched the company and found out all he could as quickly as he could. Since Bill had performed this kind of work in earlier times with great success he gained some support and enough confidence in the group to send him as the lead negotiator to gain his group's bid for control of the company.

This series of events would soon place Bill on a westbound train headed for Akron. The one overriding thought that coursed through his mind was his objective to rebuild his shattered career and regain his position on Wall Street. His new found sobriety would be the way to success and could mean the return of a comfortable life for him and his wife, Lois. Coming at this point in his life, all of this must have seemed to be heaven sent.

Unfortunately things did not turn out well for Bill and his business partners. By way of what seemed to be unscrupulous maneuvers on the part of the opposition, Bill and his associates were blindsided. Some of the votes that they had counted on were switched at the final hour leaving them with insufficient votes to have a majority. It was a nasty set of circumstances that shattered Bills vision of rebuilding his position and name in the only profession he knew[7].

Next day found the group vowing to continue the fight in the courts. Bill was left to salvage what he could of the venture and gather facts and contacts for the legal battle that was about to ensue. Bill was very low on funds but his partners promised to support his efforts while he stayed on in Akron on their behalf.

Facing a weekend alone in a city where he had no friends or anyone to share his disappointment with, he soon fell into self-pity and fierce resentment. The catastrophic results of such a promising undertaking left him feeling bitter and cheated. Fate had dealt him a bad hand and life hand turned against him once again[2].

Without his colleagues as weekend company he became lonely. By Saturday afternoon he was pacing around the lobby of the Mayflower Hotel where they were staying during the past week while the proxy fight was on.

It was at this precise moment during the midst of personal crisis that set in motion a series of events that would forever change his life and the life of countless suffering alcoholics. May 10th 1934 is the day that marks a turning point so monumentally important it is frightening to think what would have happened if Bill had chose to enter the bar at one end of the lobby. The fleeting thought had entered his mind during a particularly delicate moment, while hearing the sound of chatter and music, Bill felt drawn in. What would it hurt to have a ginger ale and perhaps strike up a conversation with a sympathetic ear? These thoughts entered the mind of an alcoholic, who on so many past occasions, had fallen prey to this kind of thinking. The thoughts were delusional and loaded with danger[11].

But, for the first time in Bills newly gained sobriety he felt panic and he knew deep inside that he was in trouble. Back in New York he remembered that he had kept sober these last five months by working with other alcoholics at Towns Hospital and Calvary Mission. This work had proven to be his protection and placed him in a position of safety.

When asked about this situation many years later he recalled, "I thought, you need another alcoholic to talk to. You need another alcoholic just as much as he needs you!" After this thought passed through his mind he quickly began his search for another drunk. At the other end of the hotel lobby he had spotted a church directory that contained a list of Akron churches and their ministers.

We can find no references anywhere to indicate that Bill Wilson considered or made any conscious effort to locate an Oxford Group minister when he looked over the names listed. It was quite at random when he chose the Reverend Walter F. Tunks. No one really knows why he picked out Tunk's although there are a few ideas as to why, but it will always remain as one of those inexplicable synchronistic events that guided him to the only minister on the list that hosted Oxford Group meetings in his church[11].

He quickly made a call to Rev. Tunks and told him of his situation and he was given a list of ten names to call. After going through the list he finally called the last name on the list a man named Norman Sheppard. Although Sheppard didn't know any drunk's, he knew a woman named Henrietta Seiberling and he knew that she had been making efforts to help a certain friend. That friend, as fortune would have it was none other than Dr. Bob

As stated earlier Bill had already met a Frank Seiberling on Wall Street and did not want to contact a person who Bill thought was his wife. Frank as it turned out had been part of Goodyear rubber and was a powerful man in the industry. Bill was afraid of contacting Frank's wife and it coming out that Bill is calling her because he is looking for an alcoholic to work with. His already tarnished name would certainly not be helped by this.

He continued to pace the hotel lobby, now even more agitated than ever. He could not get the thought out of his mind to call her. Finally in desperation he went back to his room and placed the call to Henrietta. It turned out she was not Frank's wife but his daughter-in-law. Being separated from her husband she was staying with her three children in the gatehouse of her in-laws mansion on Portage Path.

As Henrietta later would recount the story, Bill introduced himself over the phone: "I'm from the Oxford Group and I'm a rum hound from New York."

Her unspoken reaction was "this is manna from heaven" and told Bill; "You come right out here."

She was certain that this was the help that she and Anne Smith had been praying for. As it turned out Dr. Bob had recently confided in the group that he was a secret drinker. Henrietta who relied on God's guidance in her life believed that as a result of his honesty, help would arrive from where they did not know but they had faith that it would. Perhaps this visitor from New York would be that help.

It was only a month before Bill arrived in Akron that all these events took place. Because Dr. Bob didn't want attention brought to his drinking problem, the Williams' started having small private house parties at their home for Dr. Bob to help him feel more at ease. This was the very place that was to become the home to the soon to be "Alcoholic Contingent" of the Oxford Group.

What Bill brought to Akron with him was his recent success at staying sober. He also had accumulated knowledge about the disease of alcoholism by working with Dr. Silkworth at Towns Hospital in New York. In addition he had experience in working a spiritual solution to the problem that had been passed from Dr. Carl Jung to Rowland Hazard and then on to Bill by Ebby Thatcher. A linkage between the problem of alcoholism, and the solution was that "God could and would "solve the problem, if a relationship with Him was sought by using the Oxford Group's practical program of action[11].

God had truly brought to Akron the one man, completely and totally prepared, for what was about to happen. Bill Wilson was uniquely qualified to be the primary founder of Alcoholics Anonymous.

On May 11, 1935 a meeting was set up by Henrietta. The two men that would go on to found, what many have described as, the most important spiritual movement of the twentieth century, would finally meet for the first time face to face.

As time passed all the players and all of the circumstances took shape and the golden thread of synchronisticity pierced through the center of each piece of the puzzle. This amazing series of events that took years to unfold culminated in a little Midwest City, Akron, Ohio.

The Oxford Group where Bill W., Dr. Bob and others found sobriety

Bill W., Dr. Bob S., and the other "Big Book" authors, found God and sobriety in the Oxford Group. They had their spiritual awakening as the direct result of using the Oxford Group precepts of Surrender, Sharing, Restitution and Guidance.

Bill W. attended Oxford Group meetings from 1935-1937. This is where Bill worked with a long line of alcoholics and even brought some to stay in his home. When he reflected on the number of alcoholics that he had helped to achieve sobriety the count was zero. It was however noted by his wife Lois that he had remained sober throughout this time period[11].

In 1937, Bill left the Oxford Group in order to work full time with alcoholics, contrary to the desire of the Oxford Groups expectation that members work with those who had all types of problems. These Clinton St. meetings, at Bill's home, became the first AA meetings outside of the Oxford Group. However, the name Alcoholics Anonymous would not be used until the publishing of the "Big Book" in 1939.

When Bill W. left, he didn't take all the alcoholics with him. Many remained in the Oxford Group, including Rowland H., Cebra G., Victor K., and James H. among others. In fact, Dr. Bob didn't leave the Group until 1940, almost a year after the book Alcoholics Anonymous was written.
Although Rowland and others stayed in the Oxford Group, they had contact with the early A.A. fellowship through Sam Shoemaker.

Rowland H. had firsthand knowledge of the material Bill W. and the other "Big Book" authors used to write the book *Alcoholics Anonymous*. Many of those who stayed within the Oxford Group felt that the "Big Book" was Oxford Group literature written for a specific segment of the Oxford Group fellowship.

Visionary Founders gifted with Spiritual Guidance

The founders of AA were men motivated by vision, inspiration and by spiritual guidance. They knew that the unsuccessful approach that had been tried for the last 150 years, had failed, utterly, in their lives. They knew that mere abstinence alone would never work - "Why don't you be a good fellow, use your will power, and give the stuff up". They knew that by just stopping they had only scratched the surface.

The great discovery that launched AA in the first place was that the alcoholic must experience a complete and total conversion and be put into a state beyond abstinence. The real alcoholic must acquire an utterly new relationship with God. It is only then that permanent abstinence will automatically occur as a gift of grace. That was Bill's experience. That was how it happened with Dr. Bob. That was how it happened with the first one hundred members. That was how the authors of the Big Book saw it would have to happen with everyone. This fact was repeated again by Dr. William Silkworth in the Big Book, The Doctors Opinion, "unless this person can experience an entire psychic change there is very little hope of his recovery"[19].

Their experience proved to them that if they had no spiritual experience then no recovery resulted. It was also found that there were not a number of different results from working the Steps; there was only one result and this result was a spiritual experience. To the first members, spiritual experience meant that "God had touched your life and done things for you that you could not do by yourself". By the Grace of God we have been given this gift[19].

Part 5-The Founding of AA and the Origin of the 12 Steps

The Origin of the Twelve Steps

In a Grapevine article written by Bill W., entitled, "A Fragment of History", written in 1953, Bill says "AA's are always asking, where the twelve steps came from?" He goes on to say that "in the last analysis, perhaps nobody knows"[1].

It is my hope that the following will provide some insight and provide a basis for their origin. We will look back at some of the influences on Bill and show a connecting series of events, people and organizations that are at the start of our investigation. In the Book *Alcoholics Anonymous Comes of Age,* Bill writes; "Since Ebby's visit to me in the fall of 1934 we had gradually evolved "the word-of-mouth program" (page 160). Bill always gave credit for obtaining most of the basic ideas from the Oxford Group, to William James and Dr. Silkworth. We will look back and see clearly the origins of the Oxford Groups and Sam Shoemaker's ideas, as well as William James and Dr. Silkworth. In addition, the rest of the story will be uncovered as we provide connections to the twelve step ideas and where they began[2].

The program of Alcoholics Anonymous had been repeatedly described as a word of mouth program prior to the publishing of the Big Book. Another example of this can be found in the Big Book story "He Sold Himself Short" pages 290-292. In his story on page 291 the writer says, "The big A.A book had not been written and there was no literature except various religious pamphlets. The program was carried on entirely by word of mouth[9]." The religious pamphlets he was most likely talking about were the writings in a Christian weekly reader called the "Upper Room."

Dr. Bob confirms that it was a word of mouth program on pages 96 and 97 in *Dr. Bob and the Good Oldtimers[4]* in the Chapter entitled "The first group forms, In Akron" he notes "there were no Twelve Steps at the time..." (Sept. 1935). "This was the beginning of AA's "flying blind period." "They had the Bible, and they had the precepts of the Oxford Group..."[4]

As Dr. Bob recalled "I didn't write Twelve Steps. We already had the basic ideas, though not in terse tangible form. We got them... as a result of our study of the Good Book." Dr Bob goes on to say; "we must have had them. Since then we have learned from experience that they are very important in maintaining our sobriety, therefore we must have had them..." So where did they come from, if they thought they had them?[4]

For some additional clues let's look at the program that was described by Frank Amos who was sent by John D. Rockefeller to investigate what was going on in Akron to achieve the remarkable success rates (As high as 93%) that was being reported. This is what he had to say about the "self styled Alcoholic group of Akron, Ohio." Mr. Amos reported that the group all followed a similar technique and used the same system.[4] He described the "Program" in the following:

1. An alcoholic must realize that he is an alcoholic, incurable from a medical standpoint, and that he must never again drink anything with alcohol in it.
2. He must surrender himself absolutely to God, realizing that in himself there is no hope.
3. Not only must he want to stop drinking permanently, he must remove from his life other sins such as hatred, adultery, and others that frequently accompany alcoholism. Unless he will do this absolutely, Dr Bob and his associates refuse to work with him.
4. He must have devotions every morning-a "quiet time "of prayer and some reading from the Bible and other religious literature.
5. He must be willing to help other alcoholics get straightened out. This throws up a protective barrier and strengthens his own willpower and convictions.
6. It is important, but not vital, that he meet frequently with other reformed alcoholics and form both a social and religious comradeship.
7. Important but not vital, that he attend some religious service at least once weekly.[4]

He also went on to say that the members of this group are doing this program daily and also gaining new members as each day goes by. So we have the program as it was in 1935, a completely word of mouth program. Gleaned from the precepts of the Oxford Group, the Bible and as we will see shortly many other places.

Earl T., the founder of Alcoholics Anonymous in Chicago author of "He sold Himself short" pages 290-292 in *Alcoholics Anonymous*, described the six step program that Dr. Bob took him through, "he had me down to the office and we spent three or four hours formally going through the Six-Step program as it was at that time.[8]

The six steps were:
   1. Complete deflation.
   2. Dependence and guidance from a Higher Power.
   3. Moral inventory.
   4. Confession.
   5. Restitution.
   6. Continued work with other alcoholics.

This hints of the emergence of a "step program" that was evolving in the ranks of the alcoholic squadron" within the Oxford Group in 1935. However, as we will see Bill W., describes a twelve step program in his own story on pages 12-15 in the Big Book as early as 1934.
Although he does not refer to it as such, if you read carefully you can find every one of the twelve Steps. In the Big Book on page 12, paragraph 2 reads as follows:

 "My friend suggested what then seemed a novel idea. He said, "*Why don't you choose your own conception of God?*" That statement hit me hard. It melted the icy intellectual mountain in whose shadow I had lived and shivered many years. I stood in the sunlight at last.

It was only a matter of being willing to believe in a power greater than myself. Nothing more was required of me to make my beginning. I saw that growth could start from that point. Upon a foundation of complete willingness I might build what I saw in my friend. Would I have it? Of course I would!

Thus was I convinced that God is concerned with us humans when we want Him enough. At long last I saw, I felt, I believed. Scales of pride and prejudice fell from my eyes. A new world came into view. At the hospital I was separated from alcohol for the last time. Treatment seemed wise, for I showed signs of delirium tremens.

There I humbly offered myself to God, as I then understood Him, to do with me as He would. I placed myself unreservedly under His care and direction. I admitted for the first time that of myself I was nothing; that without Him I was lost. I ruthlessly faced my sins and became willing to have my new-found Friend take them away, root and branch. I have not had a drink since.

My schoolmate visited me, and I fully acquainted him with my problems and deficiencies. We made a list of people I had hurt or toward whom I felt resentment. I expressed my entire willingness to approach these individuals, admitting my wrong. Never was I to be critical of them. I was to right all such matters to the utmost of my ability.

I was to test my thinking by the new God-consciousness within. Common sense would thus become uncommon sense. I was to sit quietly when in doubt, asking only for direction and strength to meet my problems as He would have me. Never was I to pray for myself, except as my requests bore on my usefulness to others. Then only might I expect to receive. But that would be in great measure.

My friend promised when these things were done I would enter upon a new relationship with my Creator; that I would have the elements of a way of living which answered all my problems. Belief in the power of God, plus enough willingness, honesty and humility to establish and maintain the new order of things, were the essential requirements.

Simple, but not easy; a price had to be paid. It meant destruction of self-centeredness. I must turn in all things to the Father of Light who presides over us all.

These were revolutionary and drastic proposals, but the moment I fully accepted them, the effect was electric. There was a sense of victory, followed by such a peace and serenity as I had ever known. There was utter confidence. I felt lifted up, as though the great clean wind of a mountain top blew through and through. God comes to most men gradually, but His impact on me was sudden and profound.

For a moment I was alarmed, and called my friend, the doctor, to ask if I were still sane. He listened in wonder as I talked.

Finally he shook his head saying, "Something has happened to you I don't understand. But you had better hang on to it. Anything is better than the way you were." The good doctor now sees many men who have such experiences. He knows that they are real.

While I lay in the hospital the thought came that there were thousands of hopeless alcoholics who might be glad to have what had been so freely given me. Perhaps I could help some of them. They in turn might work with others.

My friend had emphasized the absolute necessity of demonstrating these principles in all my affairs. Particularly was it imperative to work with others as he had worked with me. Faith without works was dead, he said. And how appallingly true for the alcoholic! For if an alcoholic failed to perfect and enlarge his spiritual life through work and self-sacrifice for others, he could not survive the certain trials and low spots ahead. If he did not work, he would surely drink again, and if he drank, he would surely die. Then faith would be dead indeed. With us it is just like that"[9]

This part of Bills story in Chapter 1 describes his visit from Ebby Thatcher while in Townes Hospital, New York City in 1934. That shows us that the "word of mouth" program had certainly been in place and very much in use prior to Bill's arrival at the Oxford Group a few weeks later.

I think we can safely assume that it was either Rowland Hazard or Sam Shoemaker or both that had given these ideas to Ebby. Bill provides clues to this on page 39 in "When AA Came of Age".

He writes and is referring to Sam Shoemaker "It was from him that Dr. Bob and I in the beginning had absorbed most of the principles that were afterward embodied the Twelve's Steps of Alcoholics Anonymous, steps that express AA's way of life. " Bill had actually asked Sam to write the Twelve Steps for him but Sam had politely refused.

In AA Comes of Age, page 39-Bill wrote "Early AA got its ideas of self-examination, acknowledgement of character defects, restitution for harm done, and working with others straight from the Oxford Groups and directly from Sam Shoemaker"[2]

To gain further understanding of where the Oxford Groups biblical practices come from we need to look at the group's founder Frank Buchman. The Oxford Group itself was a spiritual Christian movement that had a following in Europe, China, Africa, Australia, Scandinavia and America in the 1920s and 30s. It was initiated by an American Lutheran pastor, Dr. Frank Buchman, who was of Swiss descent. In 1908 he claimed a conversion experience in a chapel in Keswick, England and later he initiated a movement called *A First Century Christian Fellowship* in 1921, and by 1931, this had grown into a movement which attracted thousands of adherents, many well-to-do, which became known as the *Oxford Group*, a name given to them by the press[5].

Three major influences that played upon Frank Buchman were his conservative Lutheran upbringing, the more traditional Protestant Evangelism which shaped a life-long interest in the process of conversion; and American evangelism of the early 20th century which traced directly to his own personal identification with Dwight L. Moody (Dwight Lyman Moody (February 5, 1837 - December 22, 1899), also known as D.L. Moody, was an American evangelist) *Remaking the world*, the title of Buchman's collected speeches, was central to Buchman's vision. In it you can see many spiritual principles that were picked up by Bill W. and the early members of AA[5].

"The Oxford Group is a Christian revolution for remaking the world. The root problems in the world today are dishonesty, selfishness and fear – in

men and, consequently, in nations. These evils multiplied result in divorce, crime, unemployment, recurrent depression and war. How can we hope for peace within a nation, or between nations, when we have conflict in countless homes? Spiritual recovery must precede economic recovery. Political or social solutions that do not deal with these root problems are inadequate".[10]

In order to "remake the world", people had to change.
"Everybody wants to see the other fellow changed. Every nation wants to see the other nation changed. But everybody is waiting for the other fellow to begin. The Oxford Group is convinced that if you want an answer for the world today, the best place to start with is with yourself. This is the first and fundamental need".[10]

Launching a campaign for "Moral Re-Armament" in East Ham Town Hall, 1938, Buchman said *"We need a power strong enough to change human nature and build bridges between man and man, faction and faction. This starts when everyone admits his own faults instead of spot-lighting the other fellow's. God alone can change human nature. The secret lies in that great forgotten truth, that when man listens, God speaks; when man obeys, God acts; when men change, nations change"[10].*

Drawing on his experiences in Penn State and China, Buchman advocated personal work with individuals that would go deep enough to deal with root motives and desires. Asked on a ship to China how he helped individuals, Buchman replied with the "five C's": Confidence, Confession, Conviction, Conversion, and Continuance. Nothing could be done unless the other person had confidence in you, and knew that you could keep confidences. Confession meant getting honest about the real state of affairs behind the public persona. This would lead to a Conviction of sin – a desire to change, leading in turn to Conversion – a decision of the will to live God's way. He felt that the most neglected "C" was Continuance, the ongoing support of people who had decided to change. One further aspect of becoming a free person was the need to make restitution – to put right, as far as possible, any wrong done (e.g. returning stolen goods or money or admitting to having told lies). Sometimes, if the sin was a public one, restitution might involve making a public confession[5].

Buchman always stressed that 'life changing' was not a matter of technique so much as the natural result of asking God for direction. God alone could change a person and the role of the "life changer" was to listen in silence for the "still small voice" of God.

Foundational to Buchman's spirituality was the practice of a daily "quiet time" during which, he claimed, anyone could search for, and receive, "divine guidance" on every aspect of their life. Because of the dangers of self-deception leading a person to mistake their own will, or shadow, for the will of God, Buchman proposed a "six-fold test" of the thoughts which came in the quiet time: 1. Look for a willingness to obey, without self-interested editing. 2. Watch and see if circumstances intervene to make the thought impractical. 3. Compare the thoughts against the highest moral standards of absolute honest, absolute purity, absolute unselfishness and absolute love. 4. Is the thought consistent with Holy Scripture? 5. Get the advice of trusted friends. 6. Draw on the experience and teaching of the Church.

The co-founders of Alcoholics Anonymous, William "Bill W." Wilson and Robert "Dr. Bob" Smith were both active members in the Oxford Group and believed that the principles of the Oxford Group were the key to overcoming alcoholism. Psychologist Howard Clinebell called Buchman "one of the foremost pioneers of the modern mutual-assistance philosophy". Swiss psychologist and author Paul Tournier said: *"The whole development of group therapy in medicine cannot all be traced back to Frank [Buchman], but he historically personified that new beginning, ending a chapter of the purely rational and opening a new era when the emotional and irrational also were taken into account.* Referring to Buchman's effect on the Church, Tournier observed: *Before Buchman, the Church felt its job was to teach and preach, but not to find out what was happening in people's souls. The clergy never listened in church, they always talked. There is still too much talking, but silence has returned. Frank helped to show again that the power of silence is the power of God".*

A review of some of the Influences on Bill in reference to the development of the Twelve Steps

As stated earlier Sam Shoemaker and his writings had a profound influence on the formation of Alcoholics Anonymous directly and indirectly by its influence on Rowland Hazard and Ebby Thatcher.

Dr. Rev. Samuel Moor Shoemaker, III, (1893–1963), was an Episcopal priest who was instrumental in the US Oxford Group HQ based in NY and founding principles of Alcoholics Anonymous. Sam Shoemaker was the rector of the Calvary Episcopal Church in New York City, which was the United States headquarters of the Oxford Group. Bill Wilson attended Oxford Group meetings at the Calvary Church and Sam was instrumental in assisting Bill Wilson with the proofreading of the book Alcoholics Anonymous

Rev. Shoemaker wrote over thirty books, at least half of which were circulating before A.A.'s 12 Steps were first published in the Big Book in 1939. Shoemaker's books were circulated in New York, Akron, and the Oxford Group.

The line of influence goes like this, in 1931 an American business executive, Rowland Hazard, sought treatment for alcoholism with psychiatrist Carl Jung:

Carl Gustav Jung (July 1875 – June 1961), was a Swiss psychiatrist, an influential thinker and the founder of analytical psychology. Jung is often considered the first modern psychologist to state that the human psyche is "by nature religious" and to explore it in depth. Jung recommended spirituality as a cure for alcoholism and he is considered to have had an indirect role in establishing Alcoholics Anonymous. Jung treated (Rowland Hazard III), suffering from chronic alcoholism. After working with the patient for some time and achieving no significant progress, Jung told the man that his alcoholic condition was near to hopeless, save only the possibility of a spiritual experience. Jung noted that occasionally such experiences had been known to reform alcoholics where all else had failed.

Rowland took Jung's advice seriously and set about seeking a personal spiritual experience. He returned home and joined the Oxford Group. He also told other alcoholics what Jung had told him about the importance of a spiritual experience. One of the alcoholics he brought into the Oxford Group was Ebby Thatcher, a long-time friend and drinking buddy of Bill W. Thatcher told Wilson about the Oxford Group, and through them Wilson became aware of Hazard's experience with Jung. The influence of Jung thus indirectly found its way into the formation of Alcoholics Anonymous[3].

The above claims are documented in the letters of Jung and Bill W., excerpts of which can be found on pages 381-386 in *Pass It On*, published by Alcoholics Anonymous. Although the details of this story are disputed by some historians, it has been documented that he was seen by Dr. Jung, the duration is however cloudy. In addition, Rowland was treated by Courtney Baylor an alcohol treatment counselor for the Emmanuel Movement between 1933 and 1934.[12]

The Emmanuel Movement was founded in 1906 by Dr. Elwood Worcester and Dr. Samuel McComb in Boston's Emmanuel Church, and in 1931 they published a book called *Mind, Body, and Spirit,* addressing the nature of alcoholism. The movement worked closely with the medical field and produced lay therapists that included Courtney Baylor and Richard Peabody. Peabody wrote *The Common Sense of Drinking,* and some of his ideas and words can be seen in the Big Book.

Bill also wrote much about the influence of William James:

William James (January 11, 1842 – August 26, 1910) was a pioneering American psychologist and philosopher who was trained as a medical doctor. He wrote influential books on the young science of psychology, educational psychology, psychology of religious experience and mysticism, and on the philosophy of pragmatism.

In the Big Book, Chapter2- There is a Solution, page 28: Bill writes "The distinguished American psychologist, William James, in his book "Varieties of Religious Experience," indicates a multitude of ways in which men have discovered God. We have no desire to convince anyone that there is only one way by which faith can be acquired. If what we have learned and felt and seen means anything at all, it means that all of us, whatever our race, creed, or color are the children of a living Creator with whom we may form a relationship upon simple and understandable terms as soon as we are willing and honest enough to try."[9]

In Appendix 2-Spiritual Experience it states:

"Most of our experiences are what psychologist William James calls the "educational variety" because they develop slowly over a period of time. Quite often friends of the newcomer are aware of the difference long before he is himself. He finally realizes that he has undergone a profound alteration in his reaction to life; that such a change could hardly have been brought about by himself alone. What often takes place in a few months could seldom have been accomplished by years of self discipline. With few exceptions our members find they have tapped an unsuspected inner resource which they presently identify with their own conception of a Power greater than themselves."[9]

The origin of influence on William James:

He was the son of Henry James Sr., an independently wealthy and notoriously eccentric Swedenborgian theologian.
The New Church (or Swedenborgianism) is the name for a religious movement developed from the writings of the Swedish scientist and theologian Emanuel Swedenborg (1688–1772). Swedenborg claimed to have received a new revelation from Jesus Christ through continuous heavenly visions which he experienced over a period of at least twenty-five years. In his writings, he predicted that God would establish a "New Church" following the Church of traditional Christianity, which worships God in one person, Jesus Christ. The New Church doctrine is that each person must actively cooperate in repentance, reformation and regeneration of one's life.

[It is an interesting fact that Lois Wilson was herself a Swedenborgian, she and Bill were married in a Swedenborgian church in New York.]

James interacted with a wide array of writers and scholars throughout his life, including his godfather Ralph Waldo Emerson a New Thought writer and philosopher. His influence from New Thought goes back to Mary Baker Eddy and Horace Dresser.

Mary Baker Eddy-Founder of Christian Science:

Bill and Lois read her book *Science and Health* aloud to one another on a trip to Vermont (A period of time in which Bill stayed sober)-*Lois Remembers* page 84. Lois goes on to say that he read and reread her book hoping thereby to strengthen his willpower. Bill also references Eddy in *Pass it On* page 230, while discussing the business structure of works publishing, it states that he studied her life as well.[6]

Other Spiritual Roots of the Twelve Steps:

So where did the term "steps" come from in describing a course of treatment? As well as other sayings such as; "Half measures were of no avail...; once a drunkard always a drunkard...;" and the story of the retired businessman; if you read *The Common Sense of Drinking* in the Table of Contents it is obvious to see what a big influence this book had on Bill Wilson in his writing of the AA Big Book.[13] In this book you will find the author (Richard Peabody) use these terms and also find the story of the retired businessman.

[Stranger than fiction: A little known synchronicity that connects Peabody and Bill W. is that both trained at the Officers Training Camp at Plattsburgh, New York, during the summer of 1917, and both were commissioned as a Second Lieutenant in the Coastal Artillery in the same unit but not during the same time period. Another little known synchronicity that exists between Bill W. and Richard Peabody is that during the same time that Bill and Lois Wilson attended Oxford Group meetings at Calvary Church in lower Manhattan, Peabody was living less than a block away at 24 Gramercy Park!]

Upon returning from World War I he (Richard Peabody) became an alcoholic. He lost his inheritance because of his drinking and his wife to an affair. After their divorce, he sought help through the Emmanuel

Movement and later wrote a book, *The Common Sense of Drinking*, in which he described a secularized treatment methodology. He was the first authority to proclaim that there was no cure for alcoholism. His book became a best seller and was a major influence on Alcoholics Anonymous founder Bill Wilson. He died of alcoholism at age 44.

Another major source of influence on Bill was a book written by Harold Begbie, *Twice Born Men*. This was a book written by Edward Harold Begbie (1871–1929), who was an English author and journalist. Begbie had a strong religious bent: he was involved in the Oxford Group and with the Salvation Army.

It is believed that Bill used the layout and format of the book, where the preface of the book describes the program and the rest of the book contains stories of alcoholics with titles like "The Puncher", "The Criminal", "The Copper Basher" and "Lowest of the Low".
In addition the author of *Twice Born Men* quotes heavily William James for example-*In the Varieties of Religious Experience*, Professor William James defines religion as the feelings, acts, and experiences of individual men in their solitude; so far as they apprehend themselves to stand in relation to whatever they may consider the divine. This definition must not be restricted to theologians and philosophers."-*Twice Born Men* page 11.[14]

Harold Begbie actually dedicated the book to William James in the following inscription:

**TO
WILLIAM JAMES
PROFESSOR OF PHILOSOPHY AT HARVARD UNIVERSITY
WITH ADMIRATION AND RESPECT**

In a Grapevine article written by Bill W., titled "A Fragment of History", written in 1953 he credits Dr. Silkworth has providing the missing link without which the set of principles now make up our Twelve Steps could never have been complete.

Dr. Silkworth contributed the very great idea without which AA could have never succeeded. For years he had described alcoholism as a disease, it was an obsession of the mind coupled with an allergy of the body that set in motion the devastating cycle of alcohol dependency. He encouraged Bill to put aside his white light experience as it sounded too crazy and told him to go after them on the medical basis first. He explained that most alcoholics won't be convinced by morals until they are certain that they must change. And the need for deflation at depth that was emphasized by William James had been neglected. We needed to be using the weight and depth of undeniable truth that medical evidence had provided. Dr. Silkworth went onto say this had never worked for him but it was his theory that an alcoholic sharing this information with another might prove to have different results. And this "missing link" was pure genius and has proven time after time to be true. One alcoholic working with another is without parallel. In the end, this proved true with the Oxford Group as well.

There were other influences that the Oxford Group had on AA, and these were due to some of the more negative features of the movement. First of all, the Group's efforts were directed to the "up and outers" rather than the "down and outers. In addition, the Oxford Group wanted Bill to work with people who had all types of worldly problems, while Bill was interested in working ONLY with alcoholics, be they Park Place or Park Bench.

Many of the alcoholics Bill was working with had trouble with the spiritual pace of the OG's four absolutes of honesty, purity, unselfishness and love. The aggressive pressure put on them to get "good overnight" was in practice a deterrent. Another problem the alcoholics had was that the non-alcoholic Oxford "Groupers" were coercing them with information the OG "team" had gained through "quiet time". The Grouper team felt they had received guidance from God and used this to give precise instructions on how the alcoholic should run his life. This could not work as the alcoholics were being told by non-alcoholics how to recover and it just did not have the depth and weight of another alcoholic sharing the very same message with them. In the end, what came out of this experience was that one alcoholic working with another was without parallel[5]. Time and time again this proved to be a universal truth not only for AA but all those who work with Alcoholics.

In Dr. Bob's own story, on page 180 in the Big Book, he said to himself, referring to Bill at their first meeting at Henrietta Seiberling's, May11,1935; "'What did the man (Bill)do or say that was different from what others had done or said?' It must be remembered that I (Bob) had read a great deal and talked to everyone who knew, or thought they knew anything about the subject of alcoholism. But this was a man (Bill) who had experienced many years of frightful drinking, who had had most all the drunkard's experiences known to man, but who had been cured by the very means I had been trying to employ, that is to say, the spiritual approach. He gave me information about the subject of alcoholism which was undoubtedly helpful. Of far more importance was the fact that he was the first living human with whom I bad ever talked, who knew what he was talking about in regard to alcoholism from actual experience. In other words, he talked my language. He knew all the answers, and certainly not because he had picked them up in his reading.[9]

This same undeniable truth, one alcoholic working with another, is illustrated in the Big Book, Chapter 2, on page 18:

"Highly competent psychiatrists who have dealt with us have found it sometimes impossible to persuade an alcoholic to discuss his situation without reserve. Strangely enough, wives, parents and intimate friends usually find us even more unapproachable than do the psychiatrist and the doctor. *But the ex-problem drinker who has found this solution, who is properly armed with facts about himself, can generally win the entire confidence of another alcoholic in a few hours. Until such an understanding is reached, little or nothing can be accomplished.* That the man who is making the approach has had the same difficulty, that he obviously knows what he is talking about, that his whole deportment shouts at the new prospect that he is a man with a real answer, that he has no attitude of Holier Than Thou, nothing whatever except the sincere desire to be helpful; that there are no fees to pay, no axes to grind, no people to please, no lectures to be endured—these are the conditions we have found most effective. After such an approach many take up their beds and walk again."[9]

To be sure, there were many influences that played on Bill and were a strong guiding force on the man who would be the primary author of the Big Book and who was also responsible for putting into words a highly successful program that would go on to save millions. The program that Bill laid out in the book *Alcoholics Anonymous* had to be transposed from a word-of –mouth program to one that could be easily read and understood perhaps by still shaky alcoholics reaching out for something that might free them from the tortures of active alcoholism.

The writing of the Twelve Steps-12 Steps in 30 minutes

As Bill sat down to write the famous fifth chapter, "How it Works", he realized he had come to a place that had been a barrier in his own mind and had caused him considerable concern. He had harbored these concerns since he began working on the book in the spring of 1938. His most dominant fear was that the message might be misunderstood by alcoholics in faraway places and this might be the only chance for recovery that those suffering might have[3]. There may literally be no "second chance at a first impression".

The basic material for this chapter was the word-of-mouth program that Bill had been using in his own recovery. The substance of this material was primarily built on Oxford Group principles and the writings of Sam Shoemaker, Frank Buchman and William James; as well as the many other sources I have identified.

Up to this point Bill had been working with Dr. Bob and the other members of the New York, Akron and Cleveland groups in testing and filtering through what had worked and what had not. While Bill would serve as the primary author of the fifth chapter, he was, by virtue of the groups' acceptance, serving as the "De facto" spokesman for all AA members.[3]

According to Bill, the word-of-mouth program that they had all had been consistently using thus far, was made up of six steps to achieve and maintain sobriety. No evidence is available or has ever been brought forth that suggests or proves that that the Oxford Group had such a program. However, the Oxford Group ideas are prevailing in these original six steps, as listed by Bill:

1. Complete Deflation.
2. Dependence on and Guidance from a Higher Power.
3. Moral Inventory.
4. Confession.
5. Restitution.
6. Continued Work with Other Alcoholics.

Bill felt that he needed to expand on these ideas and that's because they were not definitive enough, and the manipulating alcoholic may find a loophole and try to "wiggle his way out". Therefore, he went to bed one evening, while not feeling so well, at 182 Clinton Street with a pad and pencil and wrote the steps in about 30 minutes.

As was the practice of the Oxford Group, before he began he had prayed for guidance during a period of quiet time. The words came out with astonishing speed and when he was complete he counted 12 steps. He thought this a symbolic number, as he thought of the Twelve Apostles. He became convinced at this point that AA should have a 12 step recovery program.[5]

After some wrangling with the members at large, it was finally decided and the Twelve Steps, as known to all, were published in Chapter Five of the book *Alcoholics Anonymous*. And those words that we read at the start of each meeting have become immortal...

Chapter 5 How It Works

Rarely have we seen a person fail who has thoroughly followed our path. Those who do not recover are people who cannot or will not completely give themselves to this simple program, usually men and women who are constitutionally incapable of being honest with themselves. There are such unfortunates. They are not at fault; they seem to have been born that way. They are naturally incapable of grasping and developing a manner of living which demands rigorous honesty. Their chances are less than average.

There are those, too, who suffer from grave emotional and mental disorders, but many of them do recover if they have the capacity to be honest.

Our stories disclose in a general way what we used to be like, what happened, and what we are like now. If you have decided you want what we have and are willing to go to any length to get it -- then you are ready to take certain steps.

At some of these we balked. We thought we could find an easier, softer way. But we could not. With all the earnestness at our command, we beg of you to be fearless and thorough from the very start. Some of us have tried to hold on to our old ideas and the result was nil until we let go absolutely.

Remember that we deal with alcohol, cunning, baffling, powerful! Without help it is too much for us. But there is One who has all power that One is God. May you find Him now!

Half measures availed us nothing. We stood at the turning point. we asked His protection and care with complete abandon.

Here are the steps we took, which are suggested as a program of recovery:

1. We admitted we were powerless over alcohol, that our lives had become unmanageable. **The 12 Steps**
2. Came to believe that a Power greater than ourselves could restore us to sanity.
3. Made a decision to turn our will and our lives over to the care of God *as we understood Him.*
4. Made a searching and fearless moral inventory of ourselves.
5. Admitted to God, to ourselves, and to another human being the exact nature of our wrongs.
6. Were entirely ready to have God remove all these defects of character.
7. Humbly asked Him to remove our shortcomings.
8. Made a list of all persons we had harmed, and became willing to make amends to them all.

9. Made direct amends to such people wherever possible, except when to do so would injure them or others.
10. Continued to take personal inventory and when we were wrong promptly admitted it.
11. Sought through prayer and meditation to improve our conscious contact with God *as we understood Him*, praying only for knowledge of His will for us and the power to carry that out.
12. Having had a spiritual awakening as the result of these steps, we tried to carry this message to alcoholics, and to practice these principles in all our affairs.

Through the many twists and turns that Bill traveled on his path to recovery, he never gave up hope that he would find a way out. I hope that all will be convinced that no one individual invented Alcoholics Anonymous; it just grew with the help of and by the grace of God.[9]

There are Many Paths to One Fellowship...

Conclusion

By 1941, Alcoholics Anonymous was firmly established. The book *Alcoholics Anonymous* and the publishing of the infamous article in the *Saturday Evening Post* served to quadruple the membership nearly overnight. AA then was driven to focus its attention on the exponential growth of the young fellowship. Many problems that arose seemed to threaten the program; but as usual, Bill and the fellowship, worked through them with the realization that AA itself was limited. By applying the spiritual principle of acceptance to this weakness, the AA program gained strength and, once again, Bill made an asset out of a seeming liability.

Through the years 1941 to 1945 the main concern became how to share and disseminate the wisdom and experience that was quickly accumulating. Wilson feared that the establishment of a central authority might suppress further growth and limit experience. These were the conditions that led to the origination and announcement of "The Twelve Traditions of Alcoholics Anonymous". This was essential to AA's very survival as AA was soon confronted with an ever growing list of problems that would threaten AA's singleness of purpose. The influx of members with problems other than alcohol is one example of an insurmountable issue that diluted the effectiveness of previous groups.

AA and Bill soon learned that hidden in every problem lay an opportunity, however, along with the "opportunity" and what seemed to be success, might also reveal additional problems. They had to quickly learn from the unwelcome results of social acceptance and its first attempts at organizational autonomy. By 1945 many of the problems grew repetitive which served in adding a set of codified principles that offered solutions to the problems of living and working in unity. Important matters of membership, singleness of purpose, non-endorsement, professionalism, public controversy, autonomy and anonymity were addressed.

Bill feared a loss of personal touch but was soon convinced that AA must take a major growth step and take action on these pressing issues. However he stressed that "a code of traditions" could not, of course, become rule or law, but might serve as a guide for our trustees, headquarters people, and especially groups with growing pains." They were first published in the Grapevine in April 1946 as "Twelve Suggested Points for AA Tradition.

These Twelve Traditions served the fellowship well by addressing the major problems that the organization faced. The lessons learned were multifaceted yet the one essential principle within each tradition was "(AA must) make everlastingly certain that we always shall be strong enough and single-purposed enough from within, to relate ourselves rightly to the world without"[5.] This one essential principle guided Alcoholics Anonymous through many turbulent times in the next twenty five years. In the end Bill concluded and announced "May we always be willing to learn from our experience" and this was tested many times.

As Bill cautioned, in order to preserve the fellowship that so many owe their very lives to, they must continue to learn from their experiences and it is the responsibility of every member to ensure that this is done. This is why it is so important that AA remembers its history and passes this knowledge on. This was the primary motivating factor why I have written this book. Many have witnessed the straying of the fellowship and the negative influence of outside enterprises on the fellowship. Here are a few examples:

AA has strayed from where it began...

In the beginning many alcoholics of the early fellowship considered themselves to be recovered alcoholics. They felt the term "recovering" was inaccurate, as it referred to someone still struggling with the problem rather than living in the solution. "Recovering" is an expression that evolved in the 1970's as well as many other rituals and customs that are weakening the fellowship from within. Most of these "new" rituals that have developed only serve to work contrarily to the program that worked so well; as the one that Frank Amos reported to John D. Rockefeller in 1938[15].

They were recovered alcoholics, which was the term used by Bill W., Dr. Bob S. and the A.A. pioneers. The word can be found seventeen times in the first 164 pages of the "Big Book." In addition, he sometimes referred to himself as an ex-alcoholic. This expression was used in the first ten printings of the first edition of the "Big Book." In 1947, "ex-alcoholic" was changed to "ex-problem drinker."

There are many changes that have emerged since Bill passed away in 1971. You can be sure he would have had a great deal to say about them had they occurred while he was still living. Sadly many members of the fellowship have no idea how the fellowship used to be and how meetings were conducted. It is the responsibility of every member to strengthen and preserve the fellowship that has saved our lives. They must not forget to remember where they come from as a fellowship.

The early AA pioneers did not identify themselves as an alcoholic from the podium. Here again they followed the precedent set by Bill W., Dr. Bob S. and the early AA members. Neither Bill nor Dr. Bob ever identified themselves as alcoholics when speaking at A.A. meetings. To verify this all you have to do is listen to the audio tape recordings of their speeches (search the site: http://xa-speakers.org). The ritual of identifying oneself as an alcoholic, followed by a chant from the audience of "Hi _____," also came from the treatment centers; decades after the fellowship came into being. It is not a part of the "original" A.A. program.

The stating of one's name and admitting that they are alcoholic is a part of the first and fifth steps and was never meant to be a greeting or salutation. It should be a reverent and sacred moment that is filled with an attitude of self-respect and awe. By the chanting back "Hi Alcoholic" makes the fellowship, in the author's opinion, appear to be some sort of cult ritual and makes AA the butt of many a joke at the public level. AA is not a cult nor is it group therapy. As stated in the Dr's. Opinion, therapy cannot fix an alcoholic or bring about the essential spiritual conversion experience.[15]

These examples may seem trivial or even offensive to some. The main purpose of this book is not to offend, but to bring awareness to the fact that the slow insidious changes that have taken place only serve to weaken and threaten the stability of the AA fellowship. Its primary purpose can only be maintained within the structure of a unified fellowship and these listed examples only serve to threaten the unity and separate the "we" program.

It is only by having knowledge of history can AA hope to preserve the fellowship that was so freely given to suffering Alcoholics. I pray that my effort in the writing of this book serves to help in some small way.

Love in Service,
Gary Stebbings

Part 6-Flowchart of Events of significance to AA History

Condensed Flowchart of Events of Interest to Members of The Fellowship of Alcoholics Anonymous *by Miles M.*

1895 William Griffith Wilson was born Nov. 26, in a small room behind a bar in East Dorsett, VT., to Gilman and Emily Wilson.

1901 - Professor William James lectures at University of Edinburgh, Scotland. Lectures published as "The Varieties of Religious Experience" in 1902.

▸ Bill's father, Gilman, deserts the family.

▸ Bill's mother, Emily, moves to Boston and becomes an Osteopathic Physician. Bill and sister Dorothy live with maternal grandparents, Fayette and Ella Griffith.

▸ Bill's first "success" making a boomerang - "a fitting irony".

1907 - About age 12 Bill "leaves the Church" over a required temperance pledge.

1908 - Oxford Group begun as A First Century Christian Fellowship. Frank Buchman, Founder. They espoused the Four Absolutes: Honesty, Purity, Unselfishness and Love. They practiced the principles of self-survey; confession; restitution; and service to others.

1909 - Bill begins secondary education at Burr & Burton Academy.

1911 - Ebby Thatcher and Bill first met.

1912 - Bill's "first love", Bertha Bamford, dies after surgery in New York. Bill began a three year depression.

1914 - 1918, World War I

1914 - Bill enters Norwich University - a military college with strict discipline.

▸ Bill meets Lois Burnham, daughter of New York physician Dr. Clark Burnham.

1917, April 6 - U.S. enters World War I.

▸ Summer 1917 - a Second Lieutenant in the coast artillery at Ft. Rodman, Mass., Bill takes first remembered drink - Bronx Cocktail - feels a miracle - relaxed and free. A profound experience he recalled vividly more than 50 years later.

1918, January 24 - Bill marries Lois Burnham.

▸ Summer 1918 - On way to France, Bill visits Winchester Cathedral and is stirred by a "tremendous sense of presence". Reads epitaph on headstone of a Hampshire Grenadier.

▸ Nov. 11, 1918 - Armistice signed, World War I ends.

1919, January 16 - 36 states ratified constitutional amendment for prohibition.

▸ May 1919 - Bill returns home.

1920 - Bill enters Brooklyn Law School.

1921 - An investigator for U.S. F & G and also works around Wall Street.

1923, Christmas- Bill vows to stay sober one year - Lasted only 2 months.

1925-26 - Bought motorcycle and became (First?) "Market Analyst." Disease progressing.

1926 - On Wall Street full time. Disease progressing.

Late **1928** - Early **1929** - Bill crosses "invisible line" in his drinking.

1929, Oct. - Stock Market collapse.

▸ Nov. 1929 - Bill goes to Canada for a job with Dick Johnson.

1930 - 31 - Back in Brooklyn and Wall Street. Living with Lois's family - unemployed. Disease progressing.

1931 - Rowland Hazard sees Dr. Carl Jung in Zurich, Switzerland. Told no medical or psychological hope for an alcoholic of his type; told that the only hope was a spiritual or religious experience or conversion. This considered "the first in the chain of events that led to the founding of A.A."

1932, Spring - Bill's business deal in New Jersey - drank Apple Jack and drunk three days. Contract cancelled.

▸ At Towns Hospital, Bill meets Dr. William Silkworth on second admission. "The Little Doctor Who Loved Drunks."

1930-34 - Bill in "An Alcoholic Hell".

1933-34 - Bill in Towns Hospital four times.

1933, Dec. 5 - Prohibition ended.

▸ Bill resumes drinking after each admission. Disease progressing.

1934, Summer - Dr. Silkworth pronounces Bill a "HOPELESS DRUNK"

▸ Rowland Hazard returns to America and becomes involved in Oxford Group.

▸ 1934 - Emmett Fox publishes "The Sermon On The Mount".

▸ Aug. 1934 - Rowland Hazzard and Cebra persuade court to court to parole Ebby Thatcher in their custody. Ebby sobers up at Oxford Group at Calvary Episcopal Mission, where Sam Shoemaker works.

▸ Nov. 1934 - Ebby T. carries message to Bill at home. Tells his story. "One Alcoholic Talking To Another."

▸ Bill starts attending Oxford Group at Calvary Church, Bowery Mission.

▸ Bill drinks again - Back to Towns Hospital.

▸ Dec. 1934 - Bill has "Hot Flash" spiritual experience at Towns Hospital. NEVER DRANK AGAIN.

▸ Dr. Silkworth assured Bill he was not crazy; rather a "psychic upheaval" or "conversion experience."

▸ The next day Ebby brought Bill a copy of William James' "Varieties of Religious Experience".

▸ Bill reads "Varieties of Religious Experience", an explanation of need for Pain, Suffering, Calamity and "Deflation in Depth" and the "Simultaneous Transmission of Hope." The two "Halves" are joined into a "Whole."

- Bill returns to Oxford Group and works with other alcoholics, also at Sam Shoemaker's Calvary Mission and at Towns Hospital, emphasizing his "Hot Flash" spiritual experience. He noted they "seemed to do better" talking of their common problems, but no success in sobering up others.

- Bill develops belief that alcoholics are resistant to the "Four Absolutes" of the Oxford Group.

1935 - Bill, still sober, but no success yet in helping others. Still frequents Wall Street. Went to Akron Ohio for proxy fight. Lost proxy fight. Bill at Mayflower Hotel. Very discouraged and afraid he might drink.

- May 11, 1935 - Bill reached realization of: I need another alcoholic. "He starts making telephone calls. The final founding moment of A.A.

- Rev. Walter Tunks referred Bill to Norman Sheppard, and Norman referred Bill to Henrietta Seiberling, an Oxford Group adherent. She arranged a meeting the next afternoon at the Seiberling Estate with Dr. Bob Smith.

- May 12, 1935 @5:00P.M. - Bill meets Dr. Bob. Bob still drinking. Bill tells Bob of his experiences with alcohol the hopes, promises, failures told of the obsession, compulsion, and physical allergy; told him of Ebby's visit and simple message, "show me your faith and by my works I will show you mine."

- Robert Holbrook Smith. Born August 8, 1879 in St. Johnsbury, VT. Dartmouth College, Pre-Med at Univ. of Michigan. M.D. at Rush Medical college, Chicago, IL. Intern at City Hospital, Akron, OH. Proctologist. His wife, Anne was a friend of Henrietta Seiberling. They brought Dr. Bob to Oxford Group meetings for 2-1/2 yrs. and he continued to get drunk almost daily.

- Bill had presented Dr. Bob four aspects of one core idea: 1) Utter Hopelessness, 2) Totally Deflated, 3) Requiring Conversion, 4) Needing Others

- Dr. Bob understood with sudden clarity - the difference with the Oxford Group. "The spiritual approach was as useless as any other if you soaked it up like a sponge and kept it to yourself." The purpose of life was not to "get", it was to "give."

- June 10, 1935 Dr. Bob has last drink

- ALCOHOLICS ANONYMOUS IS FOUNDED

- June 11, 1935 - Dr. Bob suggests they both start working with other alcoholics.

- June 28, 1935 - Bill and Dr. Bob confront Bill Dotson, first "Man on the Bed." Bill D. was a prominent attorney in Akron. The 3rd A.A. Note: Bill D. had a spiritual experience without familiarity with Oxford Group principals.

- Henrietta Seiberling supplied them with "Infusion of Spirituality" mainly through Paul to Corinthians on "Love" and James on

- "Works" if faith is to have meaning.

- Summer, 1935 - Bill stayed in in Akron. He and Dr. Bob worked with alcoholics and attended weekly Oxford Group meetings and received spiritual nourishment.

- Fall & Winter 1935 - Back in New York on Clinton St. Hank P. and Fitz M. got sober.

Mid **1936** - a small but solid group developing at Clinton St. in New York.

► Bill's efforts with alcoholics receiving criticism from Oxford Group.

► Charles Towns offers Bill a job at Towns Hospital. Bill wanted it. The question presented to the Group and rejected because - what they had, the "thing" that bound them together and those feelings could not be bought and paid for. The only authority was the Group Conscience and all decisions were to be made by the Group.

1937 - Beginning of the split from the Oxford Group.

► Residents at Clinton St.: Ebby T., Oscar V., Russell R., Bill C., Florence R.

► Nov. 1937 - Bill and Dr. Bob meet in Akron and compare notes. Forty cases sober and staying sober. More than twenty sober for more than one year. All had been diagnosed as HOPELESS.

► A meeting of the Akron Group to consider Bill's ideas for a book, pamphlets and how to expand the movement. Presented but only narrowly passed by a majority of 2.

1938, Feb. - Rockefeller gives $5,000 and saves A.A. from professionalism.

► May 1938 - The Alcoholic Foundation established as a trusteeship for A.A.

► May 1938 - Beginning of the writing of the book Alcoholics Anonymous.

- Dec. 1938 - Twelve Steps written.

1939 - Membership reaches 100.

- April 1939 - The book Alcoholics Anonymous published.

- Summer 1939 - Withdrawal from association with Oxford Group complete. Oxford Group renamed "Moral Re-Armament."

1940 - Bill meets Father Ed Dowling who becomes his "spiritual advisor."

- "Rule No. 62."

- Feb. 1940 - First World Service January Office for A.A.

1941, March - Jack Alexander's Saturday Evening Post article published and membership jumped from 2000.

1944, January - Dr. Harry Tiebout's first paper on the subject of "Alcoholics Anonymous".

- June 1944 - The A.A. Grapevine established.

1946 - The Twelve Traditions of A.A. formulated and published. The Washingtonians in the 1840's failed, due principally to failure to adhere to "Singleness of Purpose," and this failure influenced the development of the A.A. Traditions.

1949, June 1st - Anne Ripley Smith died.

1950, July - First international convention of A.A. at Cleveland, Ohio. Twelve Traditions adopted.

▸ Nov. 16, 1950 - Dr. Robert Holbrook Smith, co-founder of Alcoholics Anonymous died.

1953, June - The book Twelve Steps and Twelve Traditions published.

1954, Oct. - The "Alcoholic Foundation" becomes the "General Service Board of A.A."

1955, July - 20th Anniversary Convention at St. Louis, MO. Second edition of Alcoholics Anonymous published.

▸ The three legacies of Recovery, Unity and Service turned over to the movement by its oldtimers.

1957 - Creation of first overseas General Service Board of A.A. in Great Britain and Ireland. A.A. Comes of Age published in

▸ October - Membership reaches over 200,000 in 7,000 groups in 70 countries and U.S. possessions.

1959 - A.A. Publishing, Inc. became A.A. World Services, Inc.

1960, July - 25th Anniversary Convention at Long Beach, CA.

1962 - Publication of Twelve Concepts for World Service written by Bill W.

1965, July - 30th Anniversary Convention at Toronto, Canada. Keynote adopted, "I Am Responsible."

1966 - Change in ratio of trustees of the General Service Board; now two-thirds majority of alcoholic members; the A.A. fellowship accepts responsibility for all it's future affairs.

1967 - Publication of the book The A.A. Way of Life now titled As Bill Sees It.

1969, Oct. 9-11 - 1st World Service meeting held in New York with delegates from 14 countries.

1970 - 35th Anniversary International Convention at Miami Beach, Florida. Keynote: "This we owe to AA's of the future. To place our common welfare first; To keep our fellowship united. For on A.A. Unity depend our lives, and the lives of those to come." Bill's last public appearance.

1971, Jan. 24 - William Griffith Wilson, co-founder of Alcoholics Anonymous, dies at Miami Beach, FL.

1972, Oct. 5-7 - 2nd World Service meeting held in New York.

1973 - Publication of Came to Believe.

▸ April 1973 - Distribution of the book Alcoholics Anonymous reached one million mark.

1975 - Publication of Living Sober.

1976 - Publication of 3rd Edition of Alcoholics Anonymous.

1988, October 5 - Lois Burnam Wilson died.

Sources:
Not God. A History of Alcoholics Anonymous by Ernest Kurtz
Alcoholics Anonymous Comes of Age, A.A. World Services, Inc.
Pass It On - Bill Wilson and the A.A. Message, A.A. World Services
The Language of the Heart, The A.A. Grapevine
Dr. Bob and the Good Old-Timers, A.A. World Services, Inc.

Part 7- Endnotes

Endnotes

The following books were indispensible in writing this book:

1. *AA Comes of Age.*
2. *Pass it On-Bill Wilson's biography*
3. *Dr. Bob and the Good Oldtimers*
4. *Not God – Ernest Kurtz*
5. *New Wine – Mel B.*
6. *Bill W. – Robert Thomsen*
7. *Lois Remembers-Lois Wilson*
8. *Alcoholics Anonymous*
9. *The Emmanuel Movement and Richard Peabody-*Katherine McCarthy, Ph.D.
10. *The Road to Fellowship-* Richard M. Dubiel
11. *The Varieties of Religious Experience-*William James
12. *The Akron Genesis of Alcoholics Anonymous-* Dick B.

And every work listed below was as well...

Introduction:

1. Why Study A.A. History?-Mitchell K.
2. In The Beginning-Mitchell K.

Part 1: Colonial America – 1618 – 1784

1. *Drinking in America: A History-*Mark Edward Lender and James Kirby Martin (The Free Press, NY 1982)
2. *Alcohol-Use and Abuse in America-*Jack H. Mendelson and Nancy K. Mello (Little Brown, Boston, 1985)
3. *The Spirits of the World-*Introduction

4. *Slaying the Dragon-The History of Addiction Treatment and Recovery in America*-William White (Lighthouse Institute Publications) 1998.
5. *Encyclopedia of World Biography* on Anthony Benezet
6. *The Jamestown Colony*-Gail Sakrai
7. *The New Americans Colonial Times-1620-1689*- Betsy Maestro
8. *The Voyage of the Mayflower*- Lassieur & Allison

Part 2- The Growing problem 1784-1872

1. *Benjamin Rush: Signer of the Declaration of Independence* (Paperback) by David Barton
2. *Symbolic Crusade: Status Politics and the Americans -* Joseph R. Gusfield
3. *American Temperance Movements: Cycles of Reform-* Blocker, Jack S. 1989
4. *Battling Demon Rum: The Struggle for a Dry America, 1800–1933*

Part 2-The Washingtonians

1. *The Washington Temperance Society of Baltimore, and The Influence It Has Had On The Temperance Movements In The United States.*
2. *The Washingtonian Movement* by Milton A. Maxwell, Ph.D
3. *The Washingtonians* - Chapter VI - The Temperance Reform and its Great Reformers
   Excerpted from The Temperance Reform and its Great Reformers by Rev. W.H. Daniels, A.M., published 1878.
4. "JOURNAL OF STUDIES ON ALCOHOL", VOL. 39 (9), 1591-1606, 1978.
   The Institutional Phase of The Washingtonian Total Abstinence Movement-Leonard U. Blumberg

5. *A.A. Tradition* - How It Developed. New York, The Alcoholic Foundation; 1947

Part 2 New Thought

1. *A History of the New Thought Movement* Horatio W. b. Dresser, 1866
2. *The Healing Wisdom Of Dr. P. P. Quimby*-Mason Clark
3. *Mary Baker Eddy*-Gill Gillian
4. *New Thought: A Practical American Spirituality*-C. Alan Anderson, Deborah G. Whitehouse
5. *As a Man Thinketh*, by James Allen
6. newthoughtlibrary.com/allenJames/bio
7. *The Creative Power in the Individual*-Thomas Troward.
8. *The Mental Cure*-Warren Felt Evans.
9. *New Thought and 12 Step Recovery From Addiction: Practical American Spiritualties*- Kenneth E. Hart
10. *The Varieties of Religious Experience*-William James
11. *The Sermon on the Mount: The Key to Success in Life* Emmet Fox
12. http://emmetfox.wwwhubs.com/
13. *The Varieties of Religious Experience*-William James
14. *Lois Remembers*-Lois Wilson
15. *Dr. Bob and the Good Oldtimers*-Dr. Bob's Biography
16. *New Wine*-Mel B
17. *Pass it On*-Bill W. Biography
18. *Not God-A History of Alcoholics Anonymous*- Ernest Kurtz

Part 2-1872-AA and the influence of Religion

1. *New Wine*-Mel B
2. biographyonline.net/spiritual/william-booth
3. *TWICE-BORN MEN* -by Harold Begbie
4. *Not God-A History of Alcoholics Anonymous*- Ernest Kurtz

Part 3 The Emmanuel Movement and AA

1. "The Emmanuel Movement and Richard Peabody",
   Katherine McCarthy, Ph.D.
   Journal of Studies on Alcohol, Vol. 45, No.1, 1984
2. "The Emmanuel Clinic, The Role of Religious Bodies in
   the Treatment of Inebriety in the United States"
   Rev. Francis W. McPeek
   Alcohol, Science and Society, 1945
3. "The Emmanuel Movement: Religion plus Psychotherapy
   From; Understanding and Counseling the
   Alcoholic", *Howard J. Clinebell, Jr.,* 1956
4. *The Road to Fellowship-The Role of the Emmanuel
   Movement and the Jacoby Club in the Development of
   Alcoholics Anonymous-*Richard M. Dubiel
5. *Remaking a Man-*Courtney Baylor
6. *The Common Sense of Drinking-* Peabody, Richard R.
7. *New Wine-*Mel B
8. http://hindsfoot.org/kdub2.html

Part 4- The Oxford Group and AA

1. *What is the Oxford Group?* published in 1933 by Oxford
   University Press, London
2. "The Oxford Group Connection"-By Ray R.
3. *Alcoholics Anonymous*
4. Bill W.'s letter to Dr. Carl Gustav Jung-Swiss psychologist
   & psychiatrist -Jan 23, 1961
5. *TWICE-BORN MEN* -by Harold Begbie
6. *Ebby-The Man Who Sponsored Bill W.*-Mel B.
7. *Not God-A History of Alcoholics Anonymous-* Ernest Kurtz
8. *Alcoholics Anonymous Comes Of Age* - A Brief History Of
   A.A. New York, Alcoholics Anonymous Publishing, Inc.;
   1957
9. *Remaking The World.* London, Buchman, Frank, N.D

10. "ROWLAND, THE MESSENGER" by Ron Ray, Bowling Green, KY
11. *Pass it On*-Bill W. Biography
12. *Dr. Bob and the Good Oldtimers*-Dr. Bob's Biography
13. *New Wine*-Mel B.
14. *The Akron Genesis of Alcoholics Anonymous*- Dick B.
15. *The Oxford Group and Alcoholics Anonymous*-Dick B.
16. *The Road to Fellowship*- Richard M. Dubiel
17. *Lois Remembers*-Lois Wilson
18. *Dr. Bob and the Good Oldtimers*-Dr. Bob's Biography
19. "Gresham's Law and Alcoholics Anonymous" by Tom P., Jr.

Part 5-The Origin of the Twelve Steps

1. "A Fragment of History", written in 1953, by Bill W.
2. *Alcoholics Anonymous Comes of Age*
3. *Pass it On*-Bill W. Biography
4. *Dr. Bob and the Good Oldtimers*-Dr. Bob's Biography
5. *Not God-A History of Alcoholics Anonymous*- Ernest Kurtz
6. *Lois Remembers*-Lois Wilson
7. "A Manual for Alcoholics Anonymous", often referred to as The Akron Manual
8. Earl T., the founder of Alcoholics Anonymous in Chicago author of "He sold Himself short" pages 290-292
9. *Alcoholics Anonymous*-3rd Edition
10. *Remaking the world*, the title of Buchman's collected speeches
11. *The Spirituality of Imperfection*-Ernest Kurtz/Katherine Ketcham
12. *The Road to Fellowship*- Richard M. Dubiel
13. *The Common Sense Of Drinking*- Peabody, Richard R.
14. *TWICE-BORN MEN* -by Harold Begbie
15. *Gresham's Law and Alcoholics Anonymous* By Tom P., Jr.

History is philosophy teaching by example and also by warning. -
Lord Bolingbroke

I would like to thank my wife Vicki for her love, support and
encouragement during some of our most trying times. She also
provided excellent editing services and put the final touch on
this book. I also want to thank my friends Professor James
Brown, Chet H., Jim D. and Fred L., for reassurance and guidance.
And finally I need to thank my children for their patience and
understanding during my long hours of writing.

www.ingramcontent.com/pod-product-compliance
Lightning Source LLC
Chambersburg PA
CBHW070144290526
45789CB00002B/623